niagara
flavours

SECOND EDITION

Recipes from Southwest Ontario's finest chefs

A Guidebook and Cookbook
BRENDA MATTHEWS
updated by Linda Bramble

James Lorimer & Company Ltd., Publishers, Toronto

James Lorimer & Company Ltd. acknowledges
the support of the Department of Canadian
Heritage and the Ontario Arts Council in the
development of writing and publishing in
Canada. We acknowledge the financial support
of the Government of Canada through the Book
Publishing Industry Development Program
(BPIDP) for our publishing activities.

We acknowledge the support of the
Government of Ontario through the Ontario
Media Development Corporation's Ontario
Book Initiative.

James Lorimer & Company Ltd., Publishers
35 Britain Street
Toronto, Ontario
M5A 1R7
www.lorimer.ca

Printed and bound in the People's Republic of China

National Library of Canada Cataloguing in Publication

Matthews, Brenda, 1953-
        Niagara flavours : recipes from
Southwest Ontario's finest chefs / Brenda
Matthews and Linda Bramble. — 2nd ed.

Includes index.
ISBN 1-55028-794-X

1. Cookery—Ontario—Niagara Peninsula.
2. Hotels—Ontario—Niagara
Peninsula—Guidebooks. 3. Restaurants—
Ontario—Niagara Peninsula—Guidebooks.
I. Bramble, Linda II. Title.

TX907.5.C22N52 2003   641.5'09713'38
C2003-903623-5

Photo Credits
Legend: Left — L; Centre — C; Right — R

Food photography by Terry Manzo, David Smiley and Dwayne Coon.
Additional photography as follows:

Page 93 — Julian Beveridge. Pages 17, 21, 23, 29, 36, 47, 53, 56, 59, 69, 76, 80, 94, 104, 108R, 110TR, 111R, 113L, 113R, 115R, 116L, 117R, 118R, 119L, 119R, 120L, 120R, 121L, 121R, 122L, 122R, 124L, 124R, 125R — Dwayne Coon. Pages 110CR, 123L, 123R, 125L — Terry Manzo. Pages 65, 107, 112L, 114, 115L — Jackie Noble. Page 100 — Nova Scotia Department of Agriculture & Marketing. Page 5 — Ontario Wine Council & Steve Elphick. Pages 87, 97 — Royal Botanical Gardens. Pages 6, 14, 63, 64, 70, 80, 109R, 110L, 112R, 116R, 117L, 118L — David Smiley. Pages 25, 111L — Brian Thompson. Page 86 — Cylla von Tiedemann. Page 57 — Keith Vaughan. Pages 7, 13, 108L, 109L — Willy Waterton.

CONTENTS

APPETIZERS. 8

SOUPS. 30

SALADS. 38

ENTRÉES. 50

DESSERTS. 82

BREADS & BREAKFAST
FOODS. 98

PROFILES. 108

INDEX. 126

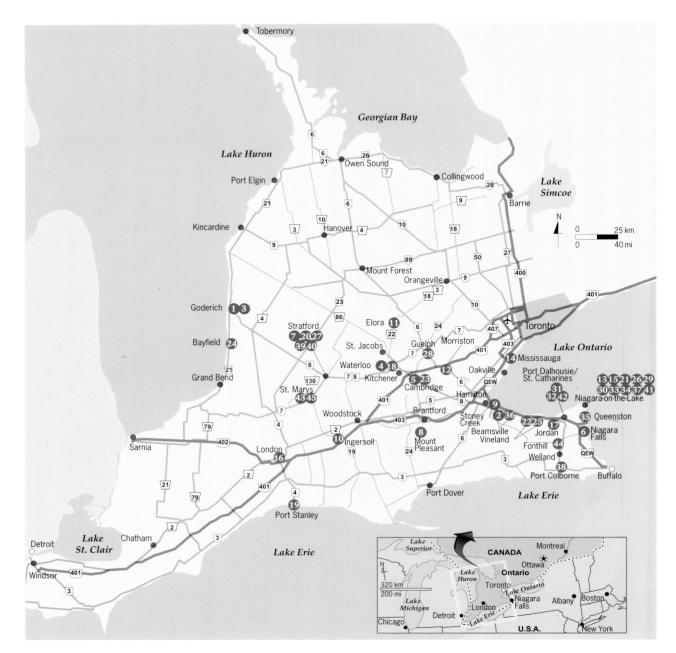

1. Bailey's Restaurant
2. The Bench Bistro at EastDell Estates Winery
3. Benmiller Inn & Spa
4. Bhima's Warung International
5. Blackshop Restaurant & Lounge
6. Casa Mia Ristorante & Bar
7. The Church Restaurant
8. Devlin's Country Bistro
9. Edgewater Manor Restaurant
10. Elm Hurst Inn
11. Elora Mill Inn
12. Enver's Restaurant
13. The Epicurean
14. Glenerin Inn
15. Hillebrand Estates Winery Restaurant
16. Idlewyld Inn
17. Inn on the Twenty
18. Janet Lynn's Bistro
19. Kettle Creek Inn
20. Keystone Alley Café
21. The Kiely Inn and Restaurant
22. Lake House Restaurant and Lounge
23. Langdon Hall
24. The Little Inn of Bayfield
25. Mark Picone at Vineland Estates Winery Restaurant
26. The Oban Inn
27. The Old Prune Restaurant
28. The Other Brother's Restaurant
29. Peller Estates Winery Restaurant
30. The Pillar and Post Inn, Spa and Conference Centre
31. Port Mansion Theatre Restaurant
32. Pow Wow, St. Catharines
33. The Prince of Wales Hotel
34. Queen's Landing Inn & Conference Resort
35. Queenston Heights Restaurant
36. The Restaurant at Peninsula Ridge
37. Ristorante Giardino
38. The Roselawn Dining Room
39. Rundles
40. Stone Maiden Inn
41. Terroir La Cachette Restaurant and Wine Bar at Strewn Winery
42. Wellington Court Restaurant
43. The Westover Inn
44. The Wildflower Restaurant
45. Woolfys at Wildwood Restaurant

PREFACE TO THE SECOND EDITION

I was pleased to be able to recommend 13 outstanding additional restaurants to Brenda Matthews' first edition of *Niagara Flavours*. Besides being endless sources of pleasurable dining, these restaurants share a keen commitment to local cuisine.

When translated onto the plate, local cuisine can reflect the diverse and captivating dishes of the people who live in the region. It can also mean cuisine created from products that are grown locally and taste wonderful because they are fresh and ripe. They are nearby, so they didn't have to be picked green, or bred to better survive transport in a shipping crate. An added bonus in Niagara is a region blessed with temperate growing conditions, which enable fruits and vegetables to ripen slowly, keeping their flavours and acidity intact. They taste better, naturally.

The restaurants listed here were also selected because of their celebration of locally made wine. Like produce grown in cooler regions, cool climate wines have the lucky feature of being the best companions with food because of their higher natural acidity and depth of flavours. The wines of Ontario have demonstrated their technical merit worldwide, as well as their elegance and distinction. All of the wines I've recommended here were made from grapes grown in Ontario and each has been selected for the complement it brings to the accompanying recipe.

Cheers!

— Linda Bramble

INTRODUCTION

From the Niagara region in the east to Huron and Bruce counties in the west, southwestern Ontario has the most agriculturally rich and productive farmland in the province. Blessed by the unique geography of the Niagara Escarpment and bounded by three Great Lakes, it is no wonder that this part of Ontario produces some of the best vegetables, fruit, farm-raised game, chicken, pork, beef and fish to be found anywhere. The bountifulness of the land, in turn, has encouraged the growth of many fine inns and restaurants whose menus showcase locally grown produce and locally sourced meats.

But as wonderful as its local cuisine may be, southwestern Ontario has more to offer than just fine dining. The Niagara region, for example, has some of the most beautiful scenery in the province as well as some of the best wineries. The quality of Niagara wines has changed remarkably since the introduction of vinifera hybrids in the 1980s. Now Niagara vintages compete with some of finest in the world.

One of the best things to do in Niagara is tour the backroads, winding through orchards and vineyards from winery to winery, sipping Rieslings, Gewürztraminers, Chardonnays, and Pinot Noirs.

Visitors can leisurely motor the countryside simply enjoying the view or they can sign up for tours, among them one that takes them bicycling with Canada's own Olympic medallist, Steve Bauer, who led the Tour de France on fifteen occasions. Niagara is also famous for beautiful and historic Niagara-on-the-Lake and for the Shaw Festival, running from April to October.

Huron and Bruce counties, sharing the Lake Huron coastline, are known for miles of sandy beaches and beautiful sunsets. They are also known as the heartland of Ontario's food production. The two pretty towns of Goderich and Bayfield both have marina facilities from May to October. Fishing boats can be seen leaving ports and bringing back freshly caught fish daily. Further east, the picturesque town of Stratford in Perth County is home to the famous Stratford Shakespearean Festival, running from May to November.

Niagara Flavours was written to be both a guide to the many fine establishments in this part of Ontario as well as a cookbook featuring the favourite creations of the region's best chefs. In selecting the recipes for this book, I have tried to provide a broad range for home use, covering the casual to the elegant, the simple to the challenging. As well, I have tried to maintain a balance of seafood, meat, and vegetarian dishes. The fine chefs with whom I worked in developing these recipes for home use all had something in common — a genuine pride and appreciation for their local farmers. In this part of Ontario, many chefs actually tour farms to select their produce, and it is not unusual to see local farmers profiled on menus. It is this abundance of fresh, local ingredients that defines this wonderfully creative and innovative regional cuisine.

Preparing this book was both fun and exciting. I greatly enjoyed visiting all the establishments and selecting the more than forty inns and restaurants that are included. The testing and sampling of the recipes was a gastronomic delight. I would like to thank the wonderful chefs, restaurateurs, and innkeepers for welcoming me into their kitchens and generously sharing their specialties. Each recipe reflects the quality and style of the establishment from which it came. I have included a chef's wine recommendation for each of the courses. I hope this will add to the pleasure of the experience.

Bon appetit and bon voyage!

— Brenda Matthews

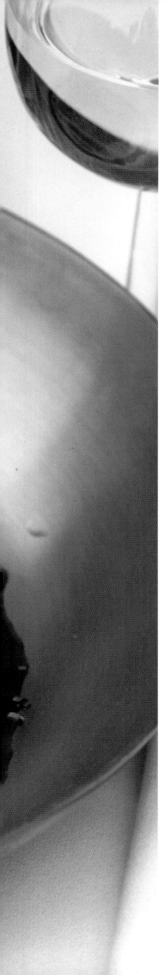

APPETIZERS

An appetizer is the first thing that guests taste when they come to your home. The first course is important because it sets the mood and whets the tastebuds for the courses that follow.

Some of the recipes included here are "finger foods," easily eaten while standing — perfect for a cocktail party. Others require a plate and fork and are more elegant appetizers, best suited as sit-down openers to a formal dinner.

This section offers a variety of delicious recipes. Some are very quick and easy to prepare like Smoked Trout Rillette from The Old Prune Restaurant. Others — Goat Cheese Soufflé with Lettuces and Marinated Vegetables from The Church Restaurant or Quail Mousseline with Balsamic Caramelized Onions and Cheese Crisps from Hillebrand's Vineyard Café — are more challenging but well worth the effort. Enjoy the exotic flavours of Thai Shrimp from Bailey's, Mussels Steamed in Thai Citrus and Coconut Broth from Wellington Court or Cha Gio from Bhima's Warung International. Many of these recipes can easily be served as a light dinner or luncheon dish by increasing the serving portion.

◀ Quail Mousseline with Balsamic Carmelized Onions and Cheese Crisps

MUSSELS STEAMED IN THAI CITRUS AND COCONUT BROTH

WELLINGTON COURT, ST. CATHARINES, ON / *Executive Chef: Erik Peacock*

These steamed mussels feature wonderful Thai flavours. Serve with a soup spoon to be sure to consume the unbelievably good broth. Chef Peacock advises keeping the mussels refrigerated until just before cooking.

3 lb	mussels	(about 75)
2 tbsp	butter	
1/2	small onion, minced	
1	clove garlic, minced	
1 tsp	minced lemongrass	
1/4 tsp	minced fresh ginger root	
1 can	coconut milk	(14 fl. oz)
2 tbsp	granulated sugar	
1 tsp	chili paste	
	juice of 1 lime	
	juice of 1 lemon	
	juice of 2 oranges	
2 tbsp	chopped fresh cilantro	

Scrub and debeard mussels. Discard any that do not close when tapped.

Melt butter in a large saucepan over medium-high heat. Sauté onion, garlic, lemongrass and ginger for about 3 minutes. Add coconut milk, sugar, chili paste and lime, lemon and orange juices. Bring to simmer; add mussels and steam, stirring once, until they open. (Discard any that have not opened.) Divide broth and mussels among 6 shallow bowls; sprinkle with cilantro. Serves 6 as a first course.

Wine suggestion — 2002 Daniel Lenko Gewürztraminer

SMOKED TROUT RILLETTE

THE OLD PRUNE RESTAURANT, STRATFORD, ON

This makes deliciously simple appetizers or hors d'oeuvres. It can be prepared in advance and refrigerated for up to four days.

2 whole smoked trout, each 1 1/2 lb

2 shallots, finely chopped

1/4 cup finely chopped mixed herbs (tarragon, chives and parsley)

3/4 cup mayonnaise

lemon juice

salt and pepper

Fillet the trout, discarding skin, head and bones. Remove fine pin bones that run the length of the fillets. Roughly crumble fillets into bowl. Add shallots, herbs and mayonnaise; stir together. Add lemon juice and salt and pepper to taste.

Divide among individual 1/2-cup ramekins or small bowls. For appetizer or light lunch: Serve with green salad and baguette. For hors d'oeuvres: Spread on small toasts or sliced cucumber rounds. Makes 4 appetizer servings, each 1/2 cup.

Wine suggestion — 2002 Cave Spring Cellars Riesling Reserve

Avon River, Stratford

THAI SHRIMP

BAILEY'S, GODERICH, ON / *Owner/Chef: Ben Merritt*

Serve these beautiful, piquant shrimp with a simple mixed green salad or cold noodle salad.

36 large shrimp, peeled and deveined (tail intact)

1/2 cup lemon juice

1/4 cup smooth peanut butter

1/4 cup fresh minced ginger root

1 tbsp olive oil

1 tsp brown sugar

1 tsp Tabasco Sauce

1 tsp curry paste (preferably Hot Patak's)

2 cloves garlic

1/4 tsp salt

1/4 tsp pepper

In food processor or blender, combine lemon juice, peanut butter, ginger root, oil, brown sugar, Tabasco Sauce, curry paste, garlic, salt and pepper; blend thoroughly. In glass or ceramic bowl, combine shrimp with marinade; let stand for 10 minutes.

Transfer shrimp to barbecue grill over medium heat; grill until just opaque. Serves 6 as a first course.

Wine suggestion — 2002 Featherstone Gewürztraminer

Countryside near Goderich

BLACKSHOP MARINATED SALMON

BLACKSHOP RESTAURANT & LOUNGE, CAMBRIDGE, ON / *Executive Chefs: Alex Vetrovsky & Ladislav Kilian*

The longer this succulent salmon is marinated, the more predominant the dill, pepper and Pernod flavours will be. The chefs at Blackshop recommend that an ideal marination time is 18 hours, but personal preference will determine yours.

3/4 cup granulated sugar

1 cup lemon juice

1/4 cup Pernod

3 tbsp salt

1 fresh salmon fillet (skin on), 3 lb

1/2 bunch fresh dill, chopped

3 tbsp crushed black peppercorns

2 lemons, cut into wedges

1 small bottle (4.4 oz) capers

1 red onion, sliced

In glass or porcelain container with edges high enough to be able to fully submerge fish in marinade, combine sugar, lemon juice, Pernod and salt.

Place fish on work surface, skin side down. Spoon marinade over skinless side. Cover with dill and peppercorns. Place skinless side down in marinade; cover tightly and let marinate in refrigerator for at least 12 hours or for up to 36 hours, turning occasionally.

To serve, slice salmon into paper-thin slices using sharp filleting knife. Fan slices on each of 10 chilled plates. Garnish with lemon wedge, capers, onion slices and sauce. Serves 10.

Wine suggestion — 1998 Henry of Pelham Pinot Noir

1/2 cup coarse Pommery (or grainy old-fashioned) mustard

1 tbsp chopped fresh dill

1 tbsp brown sugar

Sauce

Combine mustard, dill and sugar, stirring until sugar is dissolved.

Farmers' Market, Cambridge

CHA GIO

BHIMA'S WARUNG INTERNATIONAL, WATERLOO, ON / *Owner/Chef: Paul Boehmer*

Chef Boehmer says that this is one of Vietnam's most famous national dishes. These rice paper rounds can be stuffed with just about anything you like. They make excellent cocktail hors d'oeuvres. Cha gio is traditionally served with nuoc cham *dipping sauce (see recipe below).*

1 cup glass noodles

1 lb lean ground pork

1 cup salad crab

2 eggs

1/4 cup fish sauce (preferably nam pla or nuoc nam)

1 tbsp chopped fresh mint

1 tbsp chopped fresh cilantro

1 tbsp chopped Thai basil

1 tsp pepper

20 rice paper wrappers (6 inches in diameter)

2 tbsp vegetable oil

Soak noodles in warm water for about 10 minutes or until soft. Cut into 1-inch lengths.

In bowl, mix together pork, crab, eggs, fish sauce, mint, cilantro, basil and pepper. Working with 2 or 3 rice paper wrappers at a time, soak in warm water until pliable, about 1 minute. (Don't leave them too long or they will tear.)

Lay soaked wrappers on surface; spoon about 1/2 tbsp of the pork mixture just below centre. Fold over sides and roll up into cylinder. Place, seam side down, on baking sheet and cover with towel to prevent drying out. Repeat with remaining wrappers and pork mixture.

In ovenproof skillet, heat oil over medium-high heat; fry cha gio, turning occasionally until browned all over. Transfer to baking sheet and cook in 400°F oven for 10 minutes longer. Makes 20 rice paper rounds.

Wine suggestion — 2002 Hernder Estate Off-Dry Riesling

2 tbsp granulated sugar

1/2 cup warm water

1 cup nuoc nam (fish sauce)

2 tbsp lime juice

1 tbsp vinegar

1/2 tsp minced garlic

1/2 tsp chopped Thai (bird) chilies

Nuoc Cham

Dissolve sugar in warm water; stir in nuoc nam, lime juice, vinegar, garlic and chilies. Serve with cha gio.

JOE SPECK FARMS QUAIL MOUSSELINE WITH BALSAMIC CARAMELIZED ONIONS AND CHEESE CRISPS

HILLEBRAND'S ESTATES WINERY RESTAURANT, NIAGARA-ON-THE-LAKE, ON / *Executive Chef: Tony de Luca*

Chef de Luca recommends this appetizer as an ideal introduction to quail because it combines quail and chicken meat. The mousseline is very smooth and delicate. Joe Speck is a local Niagara quail farmer.

3 oz boneless chicken breast

6 oz boneless quail breast

1 tbsp butter

1 tbsp olive oil

1 leek (white part only), finely diced

5 large shiitake mushrooms (stems removed), finely diced

2 medium shallots, finely diced

1 1/2 cups 35% cream

3 1/4 cups strong chicken stock

salt and pepper

Remove skin and all sinew from chicken and quail. In skillet, heat butter and oil over medium heat; sauté leeks, mushrooms and shallots for 3 minutes. Remove from heat and refrigerate until chilled.

In food processor, purée chicken and quail until smooth. Using a pastry spatula, pass the purée through a fine strainer or sieve. Refrigerate until chilled thoroughly. Blend cream into purée. Stir in leek mixture and 1/4 cup of the stock. Season with salt and pepper to taste. Refrigerate until chilled.

Using 2 tablespoons, form quenelles from quail mousseline (see chef's tip). Bring remaining stock to boil; reduce heat and simmer. Plunge quenelles into stock; cook for about 4 minutes or until firm to the touch.

Chef's tip: To shape quenelles, set 1 metal tablespoon in bowl of hot water. Using another tablespoon, scoop out enough of the quail mousseline to fill it. Invert hot, moist spoon over filled spoon. Smoothing surface but without pressing hard, form into egg shape. After shaping, invert onto greased surface. Repeat with remaining mixture.

Hillebrand Estates Winery

Caramelized Onions

1 tsp unsalted butter

1 tsp extra-virgin olive oil

1 medium onion, julienned

2 tbsp balsamic vinegar

1 tsp finely chopped lemon thyme

salt and pepper

In small saucepan, melt butter over medium-low heat. Add oil when butter foams. Add onions and cook, stirring constantly, until glossy brown. Remove from heat. Stir in balsamic vinegar, lemon thyme and salt and pepper to taste. Let stand until mixture comes to room temperature.

Cheese Crisps

1/2 cup freshly grated Montasio, Asiago or Parmesan cheese

On nonstick baking sheet, spoon 1 tbsp of the cheese into mound. Repeat to make 7 more mounds. Bake in 350°F oven just until golden brown. Remove from oven and let cool to room temperature.

Place 2 cheese crisps on each of the 4 warmed plates. Spoon caramelized onions over cheese crisps. Top each with quail mousseline. Serves 4 as a first course.

Wine suggestion — Hillebrand Estates Trius, Brut, (Sparkling)

SMOKED CHICKEN SPRING ROLLS

THE SCHOOLHOUSE COUNTRY INN RESTAURANT, BELWOOD, ON / *Owner/Chef: Peter Egger*

Wonderfully fresh and full of flavour, these are ideal for a cocktail party.

1 cup thinly sliced Napa cabbage

3/4 cup cooked rice

1/3 cup julienned smoked chicken

2 green onions, chopped

1 clove garlic, minced

1 1/2 tbsp soy sauce

1/2 tbsp fish sauce

1/2 tbsp toasted sesame seeds

1 tsp chopped fresh cilantro

1 tsp Tabasco Sauce

1 tsp sesame oil

1/2 tsp grated fresh ginger root

10 rice paper wrappers (6 inches in diameter)

Steam cabbage very briefly. Stir together cabbage, rice, chicken, onions, garlic, soy sauce, fish sauce, sesame seeds, cilantro, Tabasco Sauce, sesame oil and ginger.

Working with 1 or 2 wrappers at a time and keeping remaining covered to prevent drying out, brush with water to moisten and place on clean cloth. Spoon filling in centre of wrapper; fold over edges and roll up to completely enclose filling. Repeat with remaining wrappers and filling. Wrap securely in plastic wrap and refrigerate until serving. Makes 10 rolls.

Wine suggestion — 2002 Inniskillin Auxerrois

DUCK CRÊPES

ELORA MILL COUNTRY INN, ELORA, ON / *Executive Chef: Randy Landry*

This is a very elegant appetizer. It's rich with wonderful flavours.

1 lb duck meat

1/4 cup sherry

pinch each chopped fresh basil and thyme

salt and pepper

3 tbsp apple chutney

phyllo pastry

1/4 cup vegetable oil

10 oz (approx) Brie cheese

Cut duck into 1- x 1/2-inch strips. Combine sherry, basil, thyme and salt and pepper to taste. Add duck strips, turning to coat; marinate for about 30 minutes.

In saucepan over medium heat, sauté duck and sherry marinade for 5 minutes or until cooked through. Reduce heat to low and add chutney; cook for 10 minutes. Season with salt and pepper to taste. Let cool.

Layer 3 sheets of phyllo pastry on top of one another. Cut to width of 2 inches. Brush with oil and top with one-tenth of the duck mixture. Cut Brie into strips and place on top. Roll up and place on baking sheet. Repeat with remaining phyllo, oil, duck mixture and Brie.

Brush crêpes with oil; bake in 350°F oven for 10 to 15 minutes or until golden brown. Place 2 crêpes on each plate. Gently heat sauce and spoon over top. Makes 10 crêpes. Serves 5 as a first course (2 crêpes each).

Wine suggestion — 2002 Cave Spring Cellars Chardonnay

1/4 cup 35% cream

1/4 cup apple cider

1/4 cup Calvados

salt and pepper

Sauce

In separate saucepan over medium-high heat, stir cream with cider and reduce by half. Add Calvados and reduce a little more. Season with salt and pepper to taste. Remove from heat.

CLOVER HONEY ROASTED QUAIL WITH PEACH GRAVY ON RUBY CHARD

THE PILLAR AND POST INN, NIAGARA-ON-THE-LAKE, ON / *Executive Chef: Virginia Marr*

Chef Marr says that this delectable appetizer recipe would also work well with pheasant. Use two pheasants and cut them in half just before serving.

3 tbsp clover honey

2 tbsp aged balsamic vinegar

salt and pepper

4 large deboned quails

4 strips European bacon*

1 bunch chard

2 tbsp herb oil

2 tbsp chopped fresh chives

Quails

In bowl, blend together honey, balsamic vinegar and salt and pepper to taste. Spread quails open and fill with rice mixture. Fold back together and wrap with bacon strips. Secure with skewer or toothpick. Glaze quails modestly with honey mixture. Roast in 375°F oven, glazing frequently, for 15 to 20 minutes or until golden brown.

Tear chard into bite-size pieces and toss with herb oil. Mound on each of 4 plates. Place quail on top and coat with peach gravy. Garnish with chives. Serves 4 as a first course.

* European bacon is a double smoked fresh bacon.

Wine suggestion — 2001 Konzelmann Golden Vintage Vidal

1 cup wild rice, cooked and chilled

4 large tiger shrimp, peeled, deveined and coarsely chopped

1 roasted red pepper, peeled, seeded and diced

1 clove garlic, minced

2 shallots, minced

2 tbsp melted unsalted butter

salt and pepper

Rice Mixture

In bowl, combine rice, shrimp, roasted peppers, garlic, shallots, butter and salt and pepper to taste. Set aside.

4 peaches, pitted, peeled and diced

2 tbsp brown sugar

3 tbsp all-purpose flour

3 cups hot chicken broth

1 sweet green pepper, seeded and diced

Peach Gravy

In saucepan over medium heat, cook peaches with brown sugar, stirring occasionally, until caramelized. Add flour and cook for 3 to 5 minutes, stirring with wooden spoon to scrape up brown bits from bottom of pan and prevent sticking. Pour in hot chicken broth 1/2 cup at a time. Add green pepper. Cook for 15 to 20 minutes or until flour is cooked out. Strain through fine sieve into another saucepan. If necessary, reduce again to achieve desired consistency.

MINI PANCAKES (POFFERTJES) WITH LAMB CROQUETTES AND BLUEBERRY CHUTNEY

MARC PICONE AT VINELAND ESTATES WINERY RESTAURANT, VINELAND, ON / *Executive Chef: Mark Picone*

Poffertjes are a traditional Dutch treat, available from street vendors on market day. This version is not the traditional sweet one, but rather savoury.

3/4 cup all-purpose flour

1 tbsp baking powder

1 tsp granulated sugar

1 tsp salt

pepper

1/3 cup milk

2 tbsp sour cream

2 tbsp olive oil

1 egg

1 tbsp finely chopped fresh rosemary

In bowl, combine flour, baking powder, sugar, salt and pepper to taste. Add milk, sour cream, oil, egg and rosemary. Stir until well combined.

Heat greased nonstick skillet over medium-low heat; using about 1 tbsp per pancake, drop batter into skillet. Cook until underside is golden brown. Turn and cook until other side is golden brown. Keep warm in oven.

Place 2 or 3 pancakes on each of 6 plates. Top with lamb croquette and blueberry chutney. Serves 6 as a first course.

Wine suggestion — 2002 Lailey Vineyards Pinot Noir

2 cups blueberries

1 cup Riesling wine

1/3 cup granulated sugar

1 cinnamon stick

Blueberry Chutney

In saucepan over medium heat, combine blueberries, wine, sugar and cinnamon stick; cook until reduced by half. Remove cinnamon stick. Let cool.

Jordan Harbour

Lamb Croquettes

3/4 lb ground lamb

1/4 cup bread crumbs

3 tbsp coarsely chopped pistachios

2 tbsp coarsely chopped dried cherries

1 egg

salt and pepper

In bowl, combine lamb, bread crumbs, pistachios, cherries, egg and salt and pepper to taste; mix thoroughly. Shape into 2-inch patties (about 3/4 inch thick) and place on baking sheet. Bake in 200°F oven for about 20 minutes. Set aside.

TOMATO BASIL TART

INN ON THE TWENTY, JORDAN, ON

This tart is the living end when the tomatoes are fresh from the field.

1 cup all-purpose flour

1/2 tsp salt

1/2 cup cold unsalted butter

ice water

Pastry

Combine flour with salt; cut in butter until mixture resembles coarse meal. Gradually pour in ice water until dough forms ball. Wrap in plastic wrap and refrigerate for 1 hour.

Roll out pastry and line 9-inch French tart pan or pie plate. Cover with foil and line with pie weights. Bake in 350°F oven for 12 minutes. Remove weights and foil.

Chef's tip: If you don't have pie weights, rice or dried beans work just as well.

Wine suggestion — 2002 Cave Spring Cellars Gamay Noir Reserve

3 to 4 medium tomatoes, cut into wedges (or 2 pints cherry tomatoes, cut in half)

1/2 cup grated Romano cheese

2 tbsp extra-virgin olive oil

2 tbsp chopped fresh basil

1 tsp chopped fresh thyme

1 clove garlic, minced

salt and pepper

Filling

Increase oven temperature to 400°F. In bowl, toss together tomatoes, cheese, oil, basil, thyme, garlic and salt and pepper to taste. Spoon into pastry shell and bake for 7 to 9 minutes or just until cheese starts to brown. (Do not overbake, as tomato juices will soften crust.) Serves 4 to 6 as a first course.

ARTICHOKE STRUDEL

DEVLIN'S COUNTRY BISTRO, MOUNT PLEASANT, ON / *Owner/Chef: Chris Devlin*

This tasty strudel can be served in large pieces for an appetizer or cut into small pieces and served as hors d'oeuvres. It can be prepared a day ahead and baked just before serving.

1 pkg (16 oz) phyllo pastry

melted unsalted butter

1 can (14 oz) artichoke hearts, drained well, sliced

10 oz (approx) shredded Asiago cheese

pepper

oil-packed sun-dried tomatoes, drained, chopped

Lay 1 sheet of phyllo pastry on work surface and brush lightly with melted butter. Fold in half. Repeat with second sheet of phyllo and lay on top of first. Place a few sliced artichoke hearts in centre; sprinkle with Asiago cheese, pepper and a few sun-dried tomato pieces. Fold edges over, tucking all ingredients under phyllo. Roll up tightly without tearing dough. Place on baking sheet. Brush lightly with butter. Repeat to make as many rolls as desired.

Bake in 425°F oven for about 12 minutes or until golden brown. Makes 10 large strudels.

Wine suggestion — 2002 Vineland Estates Dry Riesling

Devlin's Country Bistro, Mount Pleasant

GOAT CHEESE SOUFFLÉ WITH LETTUCES AND MARINATED VEGETABLES

THE CHURCH RESTAURANT, STRATFORD, ON

This great-tasting soufflé is an embellishment of the basic cheese soufflé. It captures the smells and tastes of the Mediterranean.

1 tomato

2 tbsp freshly grated Parmesan cheese

2 tbsp bread crumbs

1 1/8 cup milk

3/4 cup 35% cream

3 tbsp butter + 1 tsp

1/3 cup all-purpose flour + 1 tsp

3 egg yolks

8 oz goat cheese (chèvre)

1/2 tsp chopped fresh thyme

1/2 tsp chopped fresh oregano

5 egg whites

6 kalamata olives, pitted and diced

1 tsp lemon rind, blanched and chopped

Blanch tomato in boiling water; skin, seed and dice. Set aside. Butter ramekins. Combine Parmesan cheese with bread crumbs; line ramekins with mixture, shaking off any excess.

In saucepan, bring milk and cream to boil. Remove from heat. In separate saucepan over medium heat, melt all of the butter. Gradually add the flour and cook, stirring constantly, for about 3 minutes. Gradually add milk mixture, stirring constantly to prevent lumps. Bring to boil and reduce heat to low and simmer, stirring constantly, for 1 minute. Remove from heat.

In large bowl, cream yolks with 6 oz of the goat cheese. Blend in thyme and oregano. Gradually pour milk mixture over goat cheese mixture, whisking until thoroughly incorporated.

Beat egg whites until stiff, smooth peaks form; mix one-quarter into soufflé mixture. Fold in remaining egg whites.

Spoon into ramekins, filling about halfway. Sprinkle with some of the olives, tomatoes and lemon rind. Spoon in remaining soufflé mixture, filling almost to top. Sprinkle with remaining olives, tomatoes and lemon rind. Crumble remaining goat cheese into pea-size pieces; sprinkle on top.

Pour enough hot water into roasting pan to come 1/2 inch up sides. Place the ramekins in pan and bake in 350°F oven for 10 to 15 minutes. Let cool for 15 minutes. Shaking ramekins gently from side to side, invert onto nonstick baking sheet or sheet lined with parchment or waxed paper. (Can be refrigerated for up to 1 day.)

1/3 cup virgin olive oil

4 tsp hazelnut oil

2 tbsp white or red wine vinegar

1/2 small red onion, julienned

1/4 each sweet red and yellow pepper, julienned

1 small zucchini, julienned

1 small carrot, julienned

mesclun or mixed lettuces to serve 6

salt and pepper

Salad

Whisk together olive oil, hazelnut oil and vinegar. In nonstick skillet, heat 2 tbsp of the vinaigrette over medium heat; sauté onion, red and yellow peppers, zucchini and carrot until limp but still crisp. Let cool; add to remaining vinaigrette and salt and pepper to taste. (Can be refrigerated for up to 1 day.)

To assemble: Place soufflés on cookie sheet and heat in 375°F oven for about 10 minutes or until puffed.

Meanwhile, strain vinaigrette from vegetables, reserving vinaigrette. Toss vinaigrette with mesclun. Arrange vegetables in centre of each of 6 plates. Arrange mesclun around vegetables. Top with soufflé. Serves 6.

Wine suggestion — 2002 Creekside Sauvignon Blanc

STUFFED PORTOBELLO MUSHROOMS ON MIXED GREENS

THE PRINCE OF WALES HOTEL, NIAGARA-ON-THE-LAKE, ON / *Executive Chef: Ralf Bretzigheimer*

The mushrooms and vinaigrette can be prepared a day or two before serving this mouth-watering appetizer.

6 medium portobello mushrooms

1/4 cup olive oil

1 white onion, thinly sliced

2 tbsp port

salt and pepper

1 package fresh spinach, washed, dried and steamed

3 oz Woolwich goat cheese, sliced into 6 pieces

mesclun or mixed greens to serve 6

1/4 cup diced sweet red pepper

1/4 cup diced sweet yellow pepper

Remove stems from mushrooms and wipe caps with wet cloth.

In skillet, heat 2 tbsp of the oil over medium heat; sauté onions until caramelized and light brown. Add port and salt and pepper to taste. Set aside on small plate.

In clean skillet, briefly sauté spinach in 1 tbsp of the remaining oil until wilted; transfer to plate. Sauté mushrooms in remaining tablespoon of oil until soft.

Place mushroom caps on small baking sheet. Fill caps with caramelized onions, then 1 slice of goat cheese. Top with spinach.

Bake in 350°F oven for 5 to 8 minutes or until cheese is melted.

Meanwhile, arrange mesclun on each of 6 plates; sprinkle with diced peppers. Place heated mushrooms in centre of greens. Drizzle with vinaigrette. Serves 6.

Wine suggestion — 2002 Inniskillin Chardonnay

1/2 cup vegetable oil

1/3 cup maple syrup

2 tbsp balsamic vinegar

2 tbsp white vinegar

salt and pepper

Vinaigrette

In food processor or blender, mix together oil, maple syrup, balsamic vinegar, white vinegar and salt and pepper to taste until creamy. (You can also use a jar with a tight-fitting lid and shake vigorously.)

The Prince of Wales Hotel, Niagara-on-the-Lake

CUCUMBER GOAT CHEESE TORTE

INN ON THE TWENTY, JORDAN, ON

Serve this fresh and creamy torte with sliced hothouse tomatoes drizzled with fine quality extra-virgin olive oil.

1 English cucumber, sliced

salt and pepper

8 oz goat cheese (chèvre)

1 tsp chopped fresh basil

1 tsp chopped fresh mint

1 tsp chopped fresh chives

1/4 to 1/3 cup 35% cream

Slice cucumber thinly. Sprinkle with a little salt. Let drain in colander.

In bowl, blend together cheese, basil, mint, chives and salt and pepper to taste. Gradually stir in enough cream to soften until spreadable but not too thin.

Line bottoms and sides of 4 6-oz ramekins with cucumber slices, overlapping slightly. Divide filling equally among ramekins. Top with layer of cucumber. Refrigerate for at least 1 hour or overnight.

To serve, gently run knife along edge of ramekins and turn out onto plates. Serves 4 as a first course.

Wine suggestion — 2002 Cave Spring Cellars Off Dry Riesling

Jordan, Ontario

SOUPS

A pot of hearty soup simmering on the stove has an irresistible appeal. Filling the house with tantalizing aromas, soup is the perfect way to warm the soul on a cold and blustery day.

Served as a first course, it is an elegant and cosy way to begin a dinner party. Accompanied with a crusty loaf and salad, it makes a delicious and nourishing lunch or light dinner. And, of course, a cold soup is a lovely way to begin a summer meal.

Enjoy the bounty of the sea with Oriental Bouillabaisse from the Kiely Inn and Tapestries Restaurant or Mussel Chowder with Root Vegetables and Fresh Dill from the Westover Inn. Or refresh the palate on a warm summer day with Niagara Gazpacho from Wellington Court.

At least one or two recipes from this collection of great soups are bound to become favourites!

◀ Mussel Chowder with Root Vegetables and Fresh Dill

ORIENTAL BOUILLABAISSE

THE KIELY INN & TAPESTRIES RESTAURANT, NIAGARA-ON-THE-LAKE, ON / *Executive Chef: Vincent Sica*

Finishing with the gin and spices in this recipe adds an extra bite and unique flavour. You can make it as mild or spicy as you wish.

1/4 cup butter

1/2 cup diced carrots

1/2 cup diced celery

1 large onion, diced

2 bay leaves

1 tbsp finely chopped fresh tarragon

1 tbsp finely chopped fresh oregano

salt and pepper

4 cups puréed tomatoes

6 cups homemade fish stock or fish bouillon

1 lb mussels

8 to 10 shrimp, peeled and deveined (tail intact)

1 white fish fillet (sole, bass, cod, flounder, etc.), 8 oz

1/2 cup gin

2 tbsp lemon juice

dash Tabasco Sauce

dash Worcestershire sauce

1/4 cup chopped fresh parsley

In skillet, heat butter over medium heat; sauté carrots, celery and onions for about 8 minutes or until tender. Add bay leaves, tarragon, oregano and salt and pepper to taste; cook for 3 minutes. Mix in puréed tomatoes and fish stock; cook for 5 minutes longer. Remove bay leaves. Purée mixture in batches in food processor or blender.

Return to pot. Bring to boil and simmer for 15 to 20 minutes. Scrub and debeard mussels. Discard any that do not open when tapped. Add mussels, shrimp and fish during last 10 minutes of cooking. Add gin, lemon juice, Tabasco Sauce and Worcestershire sauce. Taste and adjust salt and pepper to taste if necessary. (Discard any mussels that have not opened.) Ladle into bowls and garnish with parsley. Serves 8 as a first course.

Chef's wine suggestion — 2000 Pillitteri Pinot Grigio

MUSSEL CHOWDER WITH ROOT VEGETABLES AND FRESH DILL

THE WESTOVER INN, ST. MARYS, ON / *Innkeepers: Julie Docker-Johnson and Stephen McCotter*

This is a deliciously rich, full-flavoured chowder that can also be enjoyed for lunch with a crusty loaf of bread. If you don't have time to make a fresh fish stock, Knorr makes a good instant seafood stock mix.

Fish Stock:

1 tsp unsalted butter

1 lb halibut bones or any white fish bones

3 1/2 cups cold water

1 small onion, chopped

1 stalk celery, chopped

1 bay leaf

6 whole black peppercorns

sprig each fresh thyme and parsley (or 1/4 tsp each dried)

salt and pepper

Chop fish bones about 3 inches long.

In skillet, melt butter over very low heat; sauté fish bones, covered, for 10 minutes. Add cold water, onion, celery, bay leaf, peppercorns, thyme, parsley and salt and pepper to taste. Simmer, uncovered, for 20 minutes. Strain through fine strainer.

Chowder:

3 cups fish stock

2 cups 2% milk

1 1/2 lb mussels (about 20)

1/2 cup white wine

salt

2 tbsp unsalted butter

2 tbsp extra-virgin olive oil

1 medium onion, diced

1 medium leek (white part only), diced

3 small carrots, diced

2 stalks celery, diced

6 new potatoes (golf ball size), cut in half

2 whole cloves garlic, smashed lightly with side of knife

1/2 tsp saffron

3 tbsp all-purpose flour

1 cup corn kernels (preferably sliced fresh from cob)

1/2 cup 35% cream

2 tbsp chopped fresh dill

1 tbsp minced garlic

salt and white pepper

In saucepan bring fish stock and milk to boil, stirring. Reduce heat and simmer, stirring, for 10 minutes; keep hot.

Meanwhile scrub mussels and remove beards. In heavy saucepan, combine mussels, wine and pinch salt; steam until mussels open. Strain, reserving liquor. Set mussels aside. (Discard any that have not opened.)

In large skillet, heat butter and oil over medium heat; sauté onion, leek, carrots, celery, new potatoes, whole garlic and saffron. Gradually stir in flour just until absorbed by butter and oil. Increase heat to high; add hot fish stock mixture, stirring constantly, until thickened.

Reduce heat and add corn, 35% cream, dill, minced garlic, and reserved liquor from mussels. Simmer just until vegetables are fork-tender. Add mussels and gently heat through. Taste and adjust seasoning with salt and white pepper if desired. Serves 6 as a first course.

Wine suggestion — 2002 Jackson-Triggs Chardonnay

ROASTED PEAR AND SWEET POTATO BISQUE WITH LOBSTER CAKES

MARK PICONE AT VINELAND ESTATES WINERY RESTAURANT, VINELAND, ON / *Executive Chef: Mark Picone*

In the early fall, when the harvest in the Niagara region is well underway, Chef Picone serves this hearty, thick, smooth-textured soup. He also suggests a variation substituting butternut squash, and salmon for the lobster. For simplicity, if you are not serving a fish cake, crème fraîche is wonderfully acidulous.

1 tbsp olive oil

1 small sweet onion, chopped

2 stalks celery, chopped

1 carrot, chopped

3 cups chicken stock

1 bay leaf

1 tsp finely chopped fresh rosemary

salt and pepper

3 sweet potatoes (unpeeled)

3 Bosc pears

6 sprigs rosemary

In saucepan, heat oil over low heat; sauté onion, celery and carrot until soft. Add stock, bay leaf, rosemary and salt and pepper to taste; cook for 25 to 35 minutes. Remove bay leaf.

Place sweet potatoes and pears on baking tray and roast in 400°F oven for about 30 minutes or until soft. Let cool. Peel potatoes and pears. In food processor, purée potatoes, pears and stock mixture in batches. Return to saucepan over low heat and simmer until heated through. Season with salt and pepper to taste.

Wine suggestion — 2002 Lakeview Cellars Dry Riesling

2 lobsters

1 cup sugar snap peas, chopped

1 sweet red pepper, chopped

1 small red onion, chopped

1 egg, beaten

3 tbsp (approx) bread crumbs

1 tbsp sour cream

1 tsp Dijon mustard

salt and pepper

1 tbsp olive oil

Lobster Cakes:

Boil lobsters. Remove meat and chop.

In bowl, combine lobster meat, peas, red peppers, onions, egg, bread crumbs, sour cream, mustard and salt and pepper to taste. Form into 6 cakes and roll in more bread crumbs.

In nonstick skillet, heat oil over medium-high heat; sear patties, turning once, until brown.

Ladle bisque into shallow soup bowls; place lobster cake in centre of each bowl and garnish with rosemary sprig. Serves 6.

CREAM OF SPINACH AND FETA SOUP

THE GLENERIN INN, MISSISSAUGA, ON / *Executive Chef: John Harnett*

Chef Harnett says that once you have made this basic cream soup, you can substitute any leaf vegetable, and a variety of cheeses may be used, including white Cheddar, yellow Cheddar and Swiss.

2 bunches fresh spinach, stems removed

1 cup homemade or canned chicken stock

2 cups 2% milk

2 cups 10% cream

1/2 cup dry white wine

1 tbsp granulated sugar

2 tsp lemon rind

salt and pepper

3/4 cup crumbled feta cheese

6 sprigs watercress

Steam spinach just until wilted. In food processor or blender, combine spinach with chicken stock; purée until smooth. Pass mixture through sieve.

In saucepan over low heat, combine spinach purée, milk, cream, wine, sugar and lemon rind. Season with salt and pepper to taste. Simmer for 15 minutes or until flavours are well blended. Pass through sieve again. (Texture should be velvety.) Return to saucepan and heat to serve.

Ladle into 6 soup bowls and sprinkle with feta cheese. Garnish with watercress. Serves 6 as a first course.

Wine suggestion — 2002 Cave Spring Cellars Dry Riesling

Cave Spring Cellars

NIAGARA GAZPACHO

WELLINGTON COURT, ST. CATHARINES, ON / *Executive Chef: Erik Peacock*

A summer delight! Cool, refreshing and full of fresh vegetables and flavour, this gazpacho can be made as mild or spicy as you wish.

4 1/2 cups tomato juice

1/4 cup finely diced sweet green pepper

1/4 cup finely diced yellow tomato

1/4 cup finely diced red onion

1/4 cup finely diced English cucumber

1/4 cup finely diced celery

juice of 1 lemon

large pinch salt

pinch white pepper

3 dashes Tabasco Sauce

2 dashes Worcestershire sauce

In bowl, combine tomato juice, green peppers, yellow tomatoes, onion, cucumber, celery, lemon juice, salt, white pepper, Tabasco Sauce and Worcestershire sauce. Refrigerate for at least 4 hours or overnight. Ladle into bowls. Serves 6.

Wine suggestion — 2002 Stoney Ridge Cellars Sauvignon Blanc

SALADS

There was a time when salad meant iceberg lettuce or — if you were really a gourmet — romaine. But times have changed. Many of the recipes featured here use a combination of lettuces varying in taste and texture, and they are tossed in an array of flavour-packed dressings. Salads have the delightful diversity of either being served as a first course to a dinner party or served in a larger portion as a main course.

The trend toward warm salads can be seen in such recipes as Warm Goat Cheese Salad and Grilled Vegetables with Roasted Garlic Dressing from Janet Lynn's Bistro, or Warm Scallop and Portobello Salad from the Schoolhouse Country Inn Restaurant. I have also included a deliciously unique Vodka Caesar Salad from the Prince of Wales Hotel.

Salads have come a long way since the days of iceberg lettuce, and the recipes included in this book show that progression.

◀ Crab Salad with Artichokes

WARM SCALLOP AND PORTOBELLO SALAD

THE SCHOOLHOUSE COUNTRY INN RESTAURANT, BELWOOD, ON / *Owner/Chef: Peter Egger*

I love delicious, easily prepared warm salads such as this one. Chef Egger suggests serving it for a light summer lunch or dinner main course. You can use shrimp instead of scallops or a combination of both.

1/4 cup olive oil

4 large portobello mushrooms, thinly sliced

1 clove garlic, minced

1 tbsp minced fresh ginger root

1 shallot, minced

20 large sea scallops, halved

1/4 cup balsamic vinegar

mixed salad greens to serve 4

1 sprig fresh thyme

salt and pepper

In skillet, heat oil over medium-high heat; sauté mushrooms, garlic, ginger and shallots until tender. Add scallops and balsamic vinegar; cook just until scallops are firm and opaque.

Arrange greens in the centre of each of 4 plates. Using slotted spoon and reserving liquid in skillet, transfer scallops and mushrooms to top of greens. Stir thyme and salt and pepper to taste into skillet and bring to boil. Cook until reduced by one-quarter. Drizzle liquid over salad. Serves 4 as a first course.

Wine suggestion — 2000 Château des Charmes Aligoté

SALAD DEANNA

THE GLENERIN INN, MISSISSAUGA, ON / *Executive Chef: John Harnett*

For a low-fat version, replace the mayonnaise and cream with low-fat plain yogurt and decrease the amount of lemon juice.

1 large head leaf lettuce

1 head radicchio

1/2 cup virgin olive oil

1/2 cup dry white wine

2 large cloves garlic, minced

1 1/2 lb medium shrimp, peeled and deveined

1 lb scallops

1 lb shark or other firm fish such as tuna or monkfish

5 kiwifruit, peeled and sliced

2 papayas, peeled and sliced

3 lemons, sliced

chopped fresh parsley

salt and pepper

Wash and dry leaf lettuce and radicchio; tear into pieces. Set aside in refrigerator.

In large skillet over medium-high heat, bring oil, wine and garlic to boil; simmer shrimp, scallops and fish for 3 to 4 minutes or until opaque. Drain seafood and keep warm in oven.

Arrange bed of greens in centre of each of 6 dinner plates; top with shrimp, scallops and fish. Arrange sliced kiwi and papaya around edge. Garnish with lemon slices and parsley. Drizzle greens, shrimp, scallops and fish with fish mayonnaise. Serves 6 as a first course.

Wine suggestion — 2001 Cilento Sauvignon Blanc Reserve

1 cup mayonnaise

1/3 cup 10% cream

3/4 cup lemon juice

2 tbsp grated onion

1/4 tsp Tabasco Sauce

Fish Mayonnaise

In bowl, mix together mayonnaise, cream, lemon juice, onion and Tabasco Sauce.

HEARTS OF ROMAINE WITH CARAMELIZED ONION VINAIGRETTE

THE KIELY INN & TAPESTRIES RESTAURANT, NIAGARA-ON-THE-LAKE, ON / *Executive Chef: Vincent Sica*

This is a delicious salad and the presentation is lovely.

6 heads romaine lettuce (or, if available, hearts of romaine only)

12 slices pancetta

8 oz Parmigiano-Reggiano cheese, thinly shaved

Wash and thoroughly dry lettuce. Collect hearts of romaine, reserving green leaves for another use.

In skillet, fry pancetta until crisp. Set aside.

Arrange romaine attractively on 6 large plates. Pour vinaigrette over leaves. Top each with 2 slices pancetta; sprinkle with Parmesan cheese shavings. Serves 6 as a first course.

Wine suggestion — 2002 Inniskillin Auxerrois

Onion Vinaigrette

1 cup olive oil + 1 tbsp

1 medium red onion, diced

4 shallots, diced

2 tbsp brown sugar

1/2 cup balsamic vinegar

salt and pepper

In nonstick skillet, heat 1 tbsp of the oil over medium-high heat; sauté onion and shallots until golden brown. Stir in sugar and remove from heat.

In slow stream, whisk remaining oil into balsamic vinegar. Add caramelized onions and salt and pepper to taste. Whisk again to blend thoroughly.

CRAB SALAD WITH ARTICHOKES

RUNDLES, STRATFORD, ON / *Executive Chef: Neil Baxter*

This is a very unique and superb-tasting salad. It features artichokes in two different ways — boiled and deep-fried into crispy chips.

9 artichokes

1 lemon, cut into quarters

4 cups corn oil

salt and pepper

1 cooked dungeness crab, 2 lb (to yield 8 to 10 oz crab meat)

4 ripe tomatoes, peeled, seeded and diced

10 basil leaves, coarsely shredded

2 cups baby salad greens

2 tbsp chopped fresh chives

Trim 6 of the artichokes, leaving some of the stalk intact. Pare down and remove choke from each artichoke. Place artichoke in water and rub with piece of lemon to expose flesh. Bring 4 cups salted water to boil; cook artichoke hearts until tender. Drain artichokes. Cut each artichoke into 6 pieces.

Toss with some of the vinaigrette.

Prepare remaining artichokes as above and let stand in water until ready to use. In deep saucepan, heat oil over medium-high heat to 325°F. Drain artichokes. Using mandoline or a sharp knife, thinly slice artichokes. Cook artichoke slices, a handful at a time, until crisp and few bubbles remain in oil. Drain well on paper towels. Season with salt and pepper to taste.

In bowl, combine crab, boiled artichoke pieces, tomatoes and shredded basil. Season lightly with salt and pepper. Dress lightly with some of the vinaigrette.

Set aside 3 tbsp of the crab mixture; divide remaining crab mixture among each of 6 plates, placing in centre and spreading out slightly. Toss salad greens with remaining vinaigrette. Arrange on plates around crab mixture. Sprinkle reserved crab mixture over greens. Sprinkle artichoke chips around salad. Drizzle orange oil in border around greens. Sprinkle with chives. Serves 6.

Wine suggestion — 2002 Cave Spring Cellars Dry Riesling

Perth County Courthouse, Stratford

Vinaigrette

1/2 cup light olive oil

3 tbsp lime juice

2 tbsp sherry vinegar

1 tbsp finely chopped shallots

1/2 tsp grated fresh gingerroot

Whisk together oil, lime juice, vinegar, shallots and ginger. Set aside.

Orange Oil

1 cup orange juice

1 tbsp lemon juice

1/4 cup extra-virgin olive oil

In non-reactive saucepan over medium-high heat, stir together orange and lemon juices; reduce until almost syrupy (about 1/4 cup). Strain through fine strainer. Add oil and whisk lightly to combine.

CANDY CANE BEET AND FETA CHEESE SALAD

WOOLFYS AT WILDWOOD RESTAURANT, ST. MARYS, ON / *Owner/Chef: Chris Woolf*

Chef Woolf is fortunate to have a local organic farm supply him with vegetables throughout the year. If you cannot get candy cane or golden beets, red beets will do.

2 lb candy cane, golden or red beets

mixed salad greens to serve 6

2 tbsp extra-virgin olive oil

1 tbsp balsamic vinegar

salt and pepper

6 oz feta cheese

chopped fresh chives

Rinse beets but do not peel. In saucepan, cover beets with cold salted water and bring to boil; boil gently just until skins can be rubbed off easily. Let cool in water in saucepan. Remove skins, trim root ends and slice.

Toss greens with olive oil and arrange on each of 6 plates. Toss beet slices in balsamic vinegar; season with salt and pepper to taste. Arrange beets over greens and crumble feta cheese on top. Garnish with chopped chives. Serves 6.

Wine suggestion — 2000 Colio Late Harvest Vidal

WARM GOAT CHEESE SALAD AND GRILLED VEGETABLES WITH ROASTED GARLIC DRESSING

JANET LYNN'S BISTRO, WATERLOO, ON / *Owner/Chef: Janet Leslie*

This fabulous salad is full of flavour. Serve for lunch with some crusty bread.

1 1/4 lb goat cheese (chèvre)

1 red onion, cut into 6 wedges

1 sweet red pepper, sliced lengthwise into 6 pieces

1 sweet yellow pepper, sliced lengthwise into 6 pieces

1 zucchini, cut into 1/2-inch-thick slices

1 eggplant, cut into 1/2-inch-thick slices

6 large mushrooms (preferably portobello), stems discarded

6 tbsp virgin olive oil

salt and pepper

1 tbsp chopped fresh thyme

torn mixed salad greens to serve 6

2 tbsp balsamic vinegar

1 tbsp chopped fresh parsley

Dipping thin knife in very hot water, cut goat cheese into 6 equal sections. Set aside.

Blanch onion wedges in boiling salted water for 2 minutes. Drain and refresh under cold water.

Arrange onions, red and yellow peppers, zucchini, eggplant and mushrooms on baking sheet; brush lightly with some of the olive oil. Season with salt and pepper to taste. Sprinkle with thyme. On grill over high heat, cook vegetables separately, about 2 minutes for peppers and about 4 minutes for the mushrooms, zucchini, eggplant and onion. While grilling, place tray of goat cheese on top rack of barbecue until warmed (not hot.)

Arrange bed of mixed greens in centre of each of 6 plates. Arrange grilled vegetables attractively around greens. Top greens with warm goat cheese. Drizzle greens and goat cheese with roasted garlic dressing. Whisk together remaining oil and balsamic vinegar; drizzle a little over grilled vegetables. Sprinkle with parsley and season with pepper to taste. Serves 6 as a first course.

Wine suggestion — 1999 Southbrook Chardonnay Triomphe

---

3 egg yolks

2 tbsp Dijon mustard

2 tbsp roasted garlic (see tip below)

1 cup vegetable oil

1/4 cup lemon juice

dash Worcestershire sauce

dash Tabasco Sauce

salt and pepper

Roasted Garlic Dressing

In food processor or blender, blend together briefly egg yolks, Dijon mustard and roasted garlic. While machine is running, gradually pour in oil. Blend in lemon juice, Worcestershire sauce, Tabasco Sauce and salt and pepper to taste. (If sauce is too thick, add a little hot water.)

Chef's tip: To roast garlic: cut bulb in half horizontally. Wrap in foil and bake in 400°F oven for 20 to 30 minutes or until very tender.

MIXED GREENS WITH POPPY SEED DRESSING

THE EPICUREAN FINE FOODS, NIAGARA-ON-THE-LAKE, ON / *Owner/Chef: Ruth Aspinall*

Chef Aspinall is constantly asked for this recipe in her restaurant but has never revealed it until now. It's an amazingly versatile recipe. In berry season, she suggests adding some fresh raspberries or strawberries for great colour and taste. For another variation, decrease the vinegar to half, add 1/3 cup lime juice and a little more sugar and serve over fresh melon with a dollop of yogurt.

3/4 cup cider vinegar

1 1/2 tbsp granulated sugar

1 1/2 tbsp poppy seeds

1 1/2 tsp (heaping) dry mustard

1 1/2 tsp salt

1 1/2 tsp (heaping) onion powder

2 cups vegetable oil

torn mixed salad greens

In food processor or blender, combine vinegar, sugar, poppy seeds, mustard, salt and onion powder; pulse a few times to blend. With motor running, gradually pour in oil until well blended. Toss with greens. Makes about 2 cups.

Wine suggestion — 2002 Henry of Pelham Rosé

The Epicurean Fine Foods, Niagara-on-the-Lake

VODKA CAESAR SALAD

THE PRINCE OF WALES HOTEL, NIAGARA-ON-THE-LAKE, ON / *Executive Chef: Ralf Bretzigheimer*

I have included two Caesar salad recipes in this collection because they are so different. This colourful, tasty one puts a brand-new twist on the old classic.

1/2 tomato baguette or regular baguette, sliced 1/4 inch thick

1/2 cup olive oil

1 1/2 heads romaine lettuce, torn into bite-sized pieces

2 tbsp finely diced tomato

2 tbsp finely diced celery

4 oz Parmesan cheese, thinly sliced

celery salt

Brush baguette slices with oil; place on a baking sheet. Bake in 300°F oven for 10 to 15 minutes or until bread is crisp.

In bowl, combine lettuce, tomatoes and celery; pour in vinaigrette and toss to coat. Arrange on plates or in shallow bowls and top with Parmesan cheese. Place toasted baguette slices alongside and sprinkle salad with a little celery salt. Serves 6.

Wine suggestion — 2000 Vineland Estates Pinot Gris

1 cup Clamato juice

1/3 cup coarsely chopped red onions

2 1/2 tsp Worcestershire sauce

1 1/2 tsp Tabasco Sauce

1 1/2 tbsp vodka

1 tsp celery salt

3/4 tsp white pepper

1/2 tsp (approx) salt

1 1/2 cups olive oil

pepper

Vinaigrette

In blender or food processor, purée Clamato juice, onions, Worcestershire sauce, Tabasco Sauce, vodka, celery salt, white pepper and salt until fine. With motor running, gradually pour in oil and blend until emulsified. Let stand for 15 minutes to develop flavours. Add pepper to taste.

ENTRÉES

Choosing the recipes for this book was truly an enjoyable experience. Each of the chefs I worked with had his or her own unique style which is reflected in the wide range of creative dishes.

Because southwestern Ontario is so bountiful, all the chefs work with their local regional producers and use only the freshest ingredients. This section includes entrées for both family meals and special-occasion entertaining. A broad range of selections is offered, including poultry, lamb, beef, pork, seafood, pasta and vegetarian dishes.

Spoil your guests with a sensational seafood dish such as Linguine Mare from da Caruso Ristorante or Grilled Tuna with Chilled Olive Salad from Benmiller Inn. On the light vegetarian side, the Cheese Soufflé from Enver's or the Grilled Vegetable and Tofu Tortes from the Wildflower Restaurant make tasty, healthy meals. Enjoy!

◀ Striped Sea Bass with Lemon Pepper Butter Sauce and Corn and Potato Risotto

STRIPED SEA BASS WITH LEMON PEPPER BUTTER SAUCE AND CORN AND POTATO RISOTTO

THE KIELY INN & TAPESTRIES RESTAURANT, NIAGARA-ON-THE-LAKE, ON / *Executive Chef: Vincent Sica*

The lemon pepper butter sauce is lovely with this delicate sea bass entrée. Instead of using frozen corn and searing in a hot pan, you can barbecue fresh corn on the cob on the grill and slice it from the cob when cooled.

6 striped sea bass fillets, each 6 to 8 oz

salt and pepper

1 cup all-purpose flour

1/4 cup vegetable oil

Sprinkle fish with salt and pepper to taste, then dredge in flour.

In ovenproof skillet, heat oil over medium-high heat; fry fish, turning once, for 2 to 3 minutes or until golden yellow.

Transfer to 450°F oven and continue cooking for 8 to 10 minutes or until opaque and flakes easily when tested with fork.

Place 1 fillet on each plate; spoon lemon pepper butter over top. Serve with potato risotto. Serves 6.

Wine suggestion — 2000 Konzelmann Pinot Blanc

1/4 cup white wine

1 tsp lemon juice

1/2 lb unsalted butter, cubed

pepper

Lemon Pepper Butter

In heavy saucepan heat wine and lemon juice over medium-high heat; reduce to about 2 tbsp. Let cool slightly.

Reduce heat to very low and whisk in butter 1 cube at a time, whisking each until well blended. Continue until all butter is blended and mixture is velvety. Pour sauce into bowl and add pepper to taste. Set aside.

8 to 10 medium Yukon Gold potatoes, peeled and diced

1 cup cooked arborio rice

2 tsp vegetable oil

1 cup frozen corn

1 cup homemade fish stock or fish bouillon

saffron (a few strands)

1 package fresh spinach (10 oz), chopped

salt and pepper

Risotto

Meanwhile, in pot of boiling water, cook potatoes until tender. Drain and set aside. Cook rice according to package directions.

In very hot skillet, heat 1 tsp oil; cook corn until appears grilled.

In separate skillet, heat remaining oil over medium-high heat, fry diced potatoes and rice for 2 to 3 minutes or until heated through. Add corn, fish stock, saffron, spinach and salt and pepper to taste; cook for 2 to 3 minutes.

Chef's tip: For a richer taste, add butter and Parmesan cheese to risotto.

FILLET OF LAKE TROUT WITH MORELS AND FIDDLEHEADS ON LINGUINE

THE LITTLE INN OF BAYFIELD, BAYFIELD, ON

This superb entrée is a grand way to enjoy fresh lake trout and fiddleheads when they're in season.

6 lake trout fillets, (small bones removed as much as possible), each 6 oz

salt and pepper

1 tbsp butter

1 tbsp olive oil

2 shallots, finely diced

18 large morels or portobello mushrooms, cut into bite-sized pieces

1 cup Chardonnay

1 cup 35% cream

1 tbsp Cognac

2 sprigs thyme

1 sprig rosemary

salt and white pepper

Season fish fillets on both sides with salt and pepper. In ovenproof skillet, heat butter and oil over medium-high heat; sear fish on both sides. Transfer to 350°F oven and bake for 15 minutes.

Add shallots to pan; cook until translucent. Add mushrooms; sauté until tender. Remove from pan.

Deglaze pan with Chardonnay. Add cream and Cognac and reduce until slightly thickened. Add mushroom mixture, thyme, rosemary and salt and white pepper to taste. Keep warm.

(Remove thyme and rosemary before serving.)

To serve, make pasta nest in centre of each of 6 plates. Place trout on top. Spoon sauce over fish, dividing mushrooms equally. Place fiddlehead mixture attractively around perimeter of plate. Serves 6.

Wine suggestion — 2000 Château des Charmes St. David's Bench Chardonnay

1 1/2 lb (750 g) linguine

1 tbsp butter

1 tbsp olive oil

1 shallot, finely chopped

1 cup chicken stock

1/2 cup 35% cream

Pasta

Cook pasta in boiling salted water until al dente. Drain and return to pot. In skillet, heat butter and oil; sauté shallots briefly. Add chicken stock and cream and cook until slightly thickened. Toss with pasta.

Fiddleheads

60 fiddleheads

2 tbsp butter

1 shallot, finely chopped

1 clove garlic, minced

salt and pepper

Blanch fiddleheads in boiling water for 3 minutes. In clean skillet, heat butter over medium heat; sauté fiddleheads, shallots and garlic until warmed through. Season with salt and pepper to taste.

GRILLED TUNA WITH CHILLED OLIVE SALAD

BENMILLER INN, GODERICH, ON

Grill the asparagus spears at the same time as grilling the tuna steak for a perfect accompaniment to this entrée.

6 tuna steaks, each 5 oz

1 cup extra-virgin olive oil

1/4 cup lemon juice

1 tbsp crushed black peppercorns

1/2 tsp garlic powder or 1 tsp chopped garlic

1/2 large red onion, diced

Combine oil, lemon juice, peppercorns, garlic powder and onion. Place tuna steaks in glass baking dish; pour marinade over top. Cover and marinate in the refrigerator for at least 1/2 hour or for up to 2 hours.

Place tuna steaks on barbecue grill over high heat; cook for 2 to 3 minutes; turn and grill for another 2 to 3 minutes or until medium-rare.

Place steaks on individual serving plates; top each with generous amount of chilled olive salad.

Wine suggestion — 2002 Angels Gate Rosé

1 cup green olives, pitted and diced

1 cup black olives, pitted and diced

1 small sweet red pepper, seeded and diced

2 garlic cloves, minced

rind (thinly julienned) and juice of 1 lemon

1 tsp dried oregano

1/2 red onion, diced

Chilled Olive Salad

In large bowl, combine green and black olives, red pepper, garlic, lemon rind and juice, oregano and onion; mix well. Cover and refrigerate to chill well before serving. Serves 6.

TROUT BAKED IN APPLE CIDER

LANGDON HALL, CAMBRIDGE, ON / *Executive Chef: Louise Duhamel*

Chef Duhamel comments that using apple cider instead of traditional wine provides a pleasant fruity flavour with a note of acidity.

2 tbsp vegetable oil

1 medium onion, cut into 1/8-inch-thick slices

1 carrot, cut into 1/8-inch-thick slices

4 trout fillets, each 6 oz

1 cup apple cider

salt and pepper

1/4 cup apple cider vinegar

2 tbsp liquid honey

2 tbsp 35% cream

1/4 cup unsalted butter

In saucepan, heat oil over medium-low heat; sauté onions until soft. Let cool. Blanch carrots in boiling water; let cool.

Place fish on greased baking pan. Top with carrots, onions, apple cider and salt and pepper to taste; cover with foil. Bake in 400°F oven for 8 to 10 minutes or until fish is opaque and flakes easily when tested with fork.

Pour juices from fish into small saucepan over high heat; cook until reduced to 1/2 cup. Add cider vinegar. Cook until reduced to 1/2 cup. Add honey and cream. Reduce again to 1/2 cup. Whisk in butter and adjust seasoning to taste.

Spoon sauce over trout to serve. Serves 4.

Wine suggestion — 1999 Strewn Two Vines Riesling Gewürztraminer

BAKED ATLANTIC SALMON WITH LEMON CREAM SAUCE AND CREAMY RISOTTO

THE WILDFLOWER RESTAURANT, FONTHILL, ON / *Owner/Chef: Wolfgang Sterr*

Chef Sterr recommends serving this salmon and risotto dish with a mixture of colourful vegetables, such as carrots, green beans, and sweet red and green peppers. For more taste, blanch vegetables, then sauté in butter and chopped fresh herbs.

6 Atlantic salmon fillets, each 6 oz

5 slices white bread

3/4 cup butter

3 tsp chopped fresh herbs (cilantro, dill, basil)

1 tsp minced garlic

1 tsp minced shallots

salt and pepper

In food processor, pulse bread until fine.

In bowl, whip butter until soft. Add herbs, garlic and shallots; mix thoroughly. Blend in bread and salt and pepper to taste.

Spread herb and garlic crust mixture about 1/2 inch thick over each salmon fillet. Bake in 450°F oven for 10 to 12 minutes or until golden brown.

Ladle lemon cream sauce on each of 6 plates; place piece of salmon on top. Spoon risotto onto each plate. Serves 6.

Wine suggestion — 1999 Willow Heights Chardonnay Stefanik Vineyard Reserve

---

1 tsp olive oil

1/2 tsp minced shallot

2/3 cup dry white wine

juice of 1 lemon

1 1/2 cups 35% cream

1/2 tsp chopped dill

salt and pepper

Lemon Cream Sauce

In nonstick skillet, heat oil over medium-high heat; sauté shallots for 1 minute. Add wine and lemon juice and reduce by half. Add cream, dill and salt and pepper to taste; bring to boil. Remove from heat until serving; warm gently.

Willow Heights Estate Winery

Creamy Risotto

2 1/2 to 3 1/2 cups vegetable stock

2/3 cup dry white wine

1 tsp olive oil

1 tsp minced garlic

1 tsp minced shallot

1 cup arborio rice

1 tbsp butter or margarine

1 tsp freshly grated Parmesan cheese

salt and pepper

In saucepan, stir stock with wine. Bring to boil; reduce heat to low and keep warm.

In large nonstick skillet, heat olive oil over medium-high heat; sauté garlic and shallots for 1 minute. Add rice and sauté for 1 minute. Add warm stock mixture 1/2 cup at a time, stirring until each addition is absorbed. Cook for 15 to 20 minutes. Rice should be creamy and firm, not runny.

Just before serving, stir in butter, Parmesan cheese and salt and pepper to taste.

SALMON MONETTE

THE CHURCH RESTAURANT, STRATFORD, ON

Salmon Monette is fresh Atlantic salmon with lemon, ginger, jasmine rice and toasted sesame seeds, wrapped in nori and steamed. It is served with pickled ginger and Japanese dipping sauce. This unique dish, a version of cooked sushi for the Western world, was presented to Richard Monette, artistic director of the Stratford Festival, for his 50th birthday celebration.

5 tbsp granulated sugar

5 tbsp rice vinegar

2 tsp salt

1 cup jasmine rice, washed

1 1/4 cups cold water

1 1/2 tbsp sesame oil

1 tbsp toasted sesame seeds

1/2 tbsp lemon rind, blanched and chopped

6 sheets nori (dried seaweed)

soy sauce

wasabi (Japanese horseradish), optional

6 skinless Atlantic salmon fillets (centre section only), each 5 oz

In saucepan over low heat, combine sugar, rice vinegar and salt; cook until sugar and salt are dissolved. Cool quickly by setting pan in cold water.

Combine rice and water in metal or glass bowl small enough to fit in large saucepan with lid. Pour in enough water to come halfway up side of bowl; bring to boil over high heat. Reduce heat to medium-low and cover. Simmer until water is absorbed and rice is cooked but still chewy and sticky. Let cool for 15 minutes. Transfer rice to large bowl. Gently stir in just enough of the sugar mixture to make rice stick together. Stir in the sesame oil, sesame seeds and lemon rind.

Brush one sheet of nori lightly with soy sauce. Smear small amount of wasabi (if using) in centre. Turn nori so that 1 corner is facing you. Spoon some of the rice horizontally across centre, leaving 1 1/2- to 2-inch border at each end. (Rice should be about 1/2 inch deep.) Place salmon fillet on top of rice. Tuck rice under salmon to make sausage shape. Fold in side corners of nori. (You will be folding over the ends of the salmon fillet.) Fold corner closest to you over salmon towards top corner. Roll up firmly. Wrap in plastic wrap.

Place salmon rolls in plastic wrap on Chinese or conventional steamer; steam gently for 15 to 20 minutes or until salmon feels firm but is still a little rare. Remove rolls and unwrap. Slicing on bias, trim into 3 pieces.

Chef's tip: Chef Russell serves this with stir-fried vegetables in the centre, with the salmon arranged around the vegetables like the spokes of a wheel, sautéed shiitake mushrooms in between and the dipping sauce ladled over the mushrooms.

Wine suggestion — 2000 Harbour Estates Riesling

2 tbsp granulated sugar

2 tbsp sherry

2 tbsp soy sauce

2 tbsp chicken stock

2 tsp rice vinegar

1 tsp sesame oil

1 tbsp cornstarch

Dipping Sauce

In saucepan, combine sugar, sherry, soy sauce, stock, vinegar and oil; bring to boil. Dissolve cornstarch in 2 tsp water and stir into pan. Reduce heat to low and simmer for 2 to 3 minutes. Serves 6.

LINGUINE WITH SHRIMPS AND SCALLOPS

THE ELM HURST INN, INGERSOLL, ON / *Executive Chef: Darrell Stewart*

This colourful pasta dish is light and fresh tasting.

1 large bunch asparagus

1 1/2 lb (750 g) linguine pasta

3/4 cup olive oil

1 lb shrimp, peeled and deveined (tail intact)

1 lb scallops

1 1/2 cups sliced wild mushrooms (shiitake, portobello or oyster)

3 small cloves garlic, minced

1/3 cup white wine

1/4 cup sliced scallions

2 tbsp chopped mixed fresh herbs (parsley, basil, thyme)

3/4 cup chopped seeded tomatoes

3/4 cup freshly grated Parmesan cheese

salt and pepper

Cut asparagus into 2-inch pieces and blanch in boiling water; set aside. In large pot of boiling salted water, cook linguine until al dente; drain and return to pot.

In skillet, heat oil over medium heat; sauté shrimp just until opaque. Remove with slotted spoon and place on warmed plate; cover with foil and set aside. Cook scallops in same manner and set aside on the same plate.

To liquid in skillet, add mushrooms, asparagus and garlic; sauté over medium heat for 1 minute. Add wine, scallions and herbs; heat through. Pour sauce over linguine; add tomatoes, Parmesan cheese and salt and pepper to taste. Toss well. Divide among pasta bowls or plates and place shrimps and scallops attractively on top. Serve with extra Parmesan cheese on the side. Serves 6.

Wine suggestion — 1999 Cave Spring Cellars Reserve Chardonnay

LINGUINE MARE

DA CARUSO RISTORANTE, ST. CATHARINES, ON / *Owner/Chef: Diana Caruso*

Chef Caruso says that variations of this dish are found throughout Italy. You can create your own by substituting different shellfish, such as manila clams or lobster.

1/2 lb each mussels, clams, scallops, shrimp and squid

1 cup olive oil

12 cloves garlic, minced

1 small onion, minced

1 cup white wine

2 cans (each 19 oz) Italian tomatoes

1 1/2 lb (750 g) linguine pasta

1/4 cup unsalted butter (optional)

1 tsp crushed chili pepper (optional)

salt and pepper

1/2 cup chopped fresh parsley

Scrub mussels and remove beards. Clean clams and scallops. Peel and devein shrimp. Cut squid into rings.

In large skillet or saucepan, heat oil over medium heat; sauté garlic and onion until translucent. Add mussels, clams and wine; cook, covered, over high heat until they open. (Discard any that do not open.) Add remaining seafood and tomatoes; bring to boil. Cook over medium-high heat for about 5 minutes or until sauce is thickened slightly.

Meanwhile, cook linguine in pot of boiling salted water until al dente. Drain and add to sauce; mix well. Stir in butter (if using), chili pepper (if using) and salt and pepper to taste. Garnish with parsley. Serves 6.

Wine suggestion — 1999 Stoney Ridge Cellars Riesling Reserve

BAKERS' CHICKEN VERMICELLI

BLACKSHOP RESTAURANT & LOUNGE, CAMBRIDGE, ON / *Executive Chefs: Alex Vetrovsky and Ladislav Kilian*

This entrée is easily prepared and tastes superb.

1/3 cup fresh bread crumbs

1 lb (500 g) vermicelli pasta, spaghettini or other pasta

1/3 cup extra-virgin olive oil

3 medium boneless skinless chicken breasts cut into 1/2 inch cubes

6 slices pancetta or bacon, sliced into 1/2 inch strips

7 cloves garlic, crushed

pinch pepper

6 medium portobello mushrooms, sliced 1/2 inch thick

2 cups chicken stock

chopped fresh herbs

Toast bread crumbs under broiler until golden. Set aside.

In pot of boiling water, cook vermicelli until al dente. Set aside.

Meanwhile, in large skillet over high heat, heat oil; cook chicken and pancetta until chicken is golden brown. Add garlic and pepper; sauté until garlic is golden brown and chicken is no longer pink inside. Add mushrooms and stock; cook over high heat for 1 minute to reduce stock. Add pasta and toss. Serve on warmed plates. Garnish with toasted bread crumbs and herbs. Serves 4 to 6.

Wine suggestion — 2000 Inniskillin Pinot Noir Reserve

Blackshop Restaurant, Cambridge

PAN-SEARED BREAST OF CHICKEN WITH BRAISED RUBY CHARD AND RHUBARB WINE

KETTLE CREEK INN, PORT STANLEY, ON / *Executive Chef: Frank Hubert*

The chicken set on top of the ruby chard is a lovely combination. The sauce is deliciously subtle. Serve with your favourite vegetable and potato.

1/4 cup extra-virgin olive oil

6 boneless skinless chicken breasts, each 6 oz

1 large bunch ruby chard or Swiss chard

1 1/8 cups rhubarb wine* or dry pink Zinfandel

1/2 cup unsalted butter

1 tbsp crushed black peppercorns

2 tbsp chopped shallots

* Rhubarb wine is produced by Quai du Vin Winery, a local winery

In large nonstick skillet, heat oil over medium-high heat; sear chicken until golden brown.

Wash, dry and shred chard. Place in small roasting pan along with chicken and half of the wine. Roast, covered, in 400°F oven for about 10 minutes or until chicken is no longer pink inside. Transfer chicken and chard to plate and keep warm. Place pan over medium-high heat; pour in remaining wine and cook until reduced by half. Whisk in butter, peppercorns and shallots. Remove from heat.

Divide chard among 6 plates; place chicken breasts on top and pour sauce over top. Serves 6.

Wine suggestion — Harvest Estates Strawberry Rhubarb

Kettle Creek Inn, Port Stanley

GRAIN-FED CHICKEN WITH HERBED CREAM CHEESE AND FRESH TOMATO SAUCE

KEYSTONE ALLEY CAFÉ, STRATFORD, ON / *Owner/Chef: Sheldon Russell*

Chef Russell serves this delicious chicken with porcini mushroom risotto and grilled mixed vegetables.

6 grain-fed boneless chicken breasts (skin on), each 7 oz

9 oz cream cheese

1/2 cup chopped mixed fresh herbs (tarragon, thyme, parsley, oregano, chives and chervil)

2 tbsp olive oil

salt and pepper

Place 1 chicken breast skin side down on work surface. Using sharp knife, remove fillet. Make shallow incision lengthwise along breast. Carefully work knife toward sides of breasts without cutting completely. Make horizontal incisions along top and bottom of lengthwise incision, creating flaps. Open up flaps. Gently flatten chicken between 2 pieces of plastic wrap, being careful not to separate. In same manner, flatten fillet. Repeat with remaining chicken breasts.

In food processor, blend cream cheese with herbs until smooth.

Spoon equal amounts of cream cheese mixture along centre of each breast, shaping lengthwise. Place slightly flattened fillet on top. To close, pull flaps over fillet.

In large nonstick skillet, heat oil over medium-high heat; place chicken in skillet, skin side down, and brown on 1 side only. Transfer, skin side up, to ovenproof platter or baking sheet; roast in 375°F oven for 20 to 25 minutes or until no longer pink inside. Let stand for 10 minutes.

Wine suggestion — 2001 Thomas & Vaughan Pinot Gris

---

1 tbsp olive oil

4 shallots, chopped

2 cloves garlic, crushed

7 fresh ripe tomatoes, seeded and chopped

1/2 cup dry white wine

1/4 cup chicken stock

6 oregano leaves, chopped

1 sprig each thyme and tarragon

1/2 bay leaf

salt and pepper

Fresh Tomato Sauce

Meanwhile, in skillet, heat oil over medium heat; sauté shallots until soft. Add garlic and cook for 1 minute. Add tomatoes, wine, stock, oregano, thyme, tarragon, bay leaf and salt and pepper to taste; cook for 15 to 20 minutes. Discard sprigs of thyme and tarragon and bay leaf. Spoon over chicken to serve. Serves 6.

BREAST OF CHICKEN WITH GOAT CHEESE AND SUN-DRIED TOMATO JUS

WOOLFYS AT WILDWOOD RESTAURANT, ST. MARYS, ON / *Owner/Chef: Chris Woolf*

Chef Woolf suggests serving potatoes and sautéed spinach with this scrumptious chicken entrée.

6 boneless chicken breasts (skin on), each 6 oz

1 tbsp basil pesto (homemade or purchased)

6 oz goat cheese

3 tbsp olive oil

1/2 cup dry white wine

1 cup strong chicken stock

4 tbsp cold unsalted butter

2 tbsp chopped oil-packed sun-dried tomatoes

Place 1 chicken breast skin side down on work surface. Using sharp knife, remove fillet. Make shallow incision lengthwise along breast. Carefully work knife toward sides of breast without cutting completely. Make horizontal incisions along top and bottom of lengthwise incision, creating flaps. Open up flaps. Gently flatten fillet between 2 pieces of plastic wrap. Repeat with remaining chicken breasts.

Spread pesto on inside of chicken breasts. Place 1 oz of goat cheese in centre of each breast, shaping lengthwise. Place slightly flattened fillet on top. To close, pull flaps over fillet.

In large ovenproof skillet, heat 2 tbsp of the oil over high heat. Brush skinless side of breasts with remaining oil. Place breasts in skillet, skin side down, and brown lightly on 1 side only. Transfer to top rack of 375°F oven and cook for about 15 minutes or until no longer pink inside. Remove from skillet and keep warm.

Meanwhile, drain fat from skillet. Deglaze skillet with wine; cook until reduced by one-quarter. Add stock and reduce by another one-quarter. While still boiling, whisk in butter, then remove from heat. Pass through strainer into bowl. Toss in sun-dried tomatoes. To serve, spoon sauce over chicken breasts. Serves 6.

Wine suggestion — 2000 Malivoire Wine Company Chardonnay

BARBECUED BREAST OF DUCK ACCENTED WITH COCONUT & ACCOMPANIED WITH GRILLED VEGETABLES

BENMILLER INN, GODERICH, ON

The Benmiller Inn recommends serving this duck dish with its fabulous barbecue sauce and grilled vegetables. The barbecue sauce also goes well with salmon or any kind of meat or poultry. The recipe makes about 4 cups of sauce, which can be refrigerated in a tightly sealed container for up to 4 weeks. You may also want to freeze it in small freezer bags to thaw as needed. Grill duck only until medium-rare; if cooked longer it will become tough.

1 bunch asparagus

1 eggplant, cut into large cubes

1 sweet red pepper, coarsely chopped

1 sweet green pepper, coarsely chopped

1 red onion, cut into 8 sections

6 boneless skinless duck breasts, each 6 oz

toasted unsweetened coconut

Cut each asparagus spear in half lengthwise. In bowl, combine asparagus, eggplant, red and green peppers and onion; toss with 1/4 cup of the vegetable basting sauce. Place vegetables in grilling basket over medium-high heat; cook, turning basket occasionally and basting regularly with remaining sauce, for about 10 minutes or until tender.

Meanwhile, place duck breasts on grill; cook, basting regularly with barbecue sauce, for about 5 minutes per side or until medium-rare.

To serve, carefully slice breasts into thin strips and arrange on serving platter in star pattern. Divide grilled vegetables among plates. Sprinkle with toasted coconut. Serves 6.

Wine suggestion — 2000 Henry of Pelham Special Select Late Harvest Vidal

1/2 cup butter, diced

1/3 cup olive oil

3 tbsp Dijon mustard

1 tbsp grated lemon rind

2 tbsp lemon juice

2 tbsp chopped fresh thyme

Vegetable Basting Sauce

In small saucepan, combine butter, oil, mustard, lemon rind and juice and thyme; bring to simmer and set aside.

Benmiller Inn's Barbecue Sauce

2 cups chopped onions

1/2 cup vegetable oil

1/4 cup minced garlic

1 1/2 tbsp ground cumin

1 tsp cayenne pepper

2 cups ketchup

1/2 cup balsamic vinegar

1/2 cup soy sauce

1/3 cup brown sugar

1/4 cup red wine vinegar

1/4 cup Worcestershire sauce

1 tsp Tabasco Sauce

In blender or food processor, purée together onions, oil, garlic, cumin and cayenne; sauté in saucepan over medium-low heat until soft. Add ketchup, balsamic vinegar, soy sauce, brown sugar, red wine vinegar, Worcestershire sauce and Tabasco Sauce; stir until blended. Reduce heat to low and simmer for 4 to 6 hours.

BEBEK BETUTU (ROAST DUCK)

BHIMA'S WARUNG INTERNATIONAL, WATERLOO, ON / *Owner/Chef: Paul Boehmer*

On the island of Bali, Indonesia, this dish is reserved for special occasions and cooked slowly all day by burying the packaged bird in the sand and building a fire out of coconut husks on top of it. The fresh spices and banana leaves are available in southeast Asian grocery stores. Chef Boehmer suggests accompanying this full-flavoured duck with a sweet and sour fruit sauce. Tamarind peach works well with the richness of the dish. He also recommends serving it with simple steamed Thai rice and a green vegetable such as spinach.

1 cup ground candlenuts or almonds

1 tbsp fresh turmeric

1 tbsp finely grated fresh galangal

1 tbsp finely grated fresh lemongrass

1 tbsp minced garlic

1 tbsp chopped shallots

1 tsp chopped Thai (bird) chilies

1 tsp ground coriander seeds

1 tsp nutmeg

1 tsp cinnamon

1/2 tsp ground cloves

1/2 tsp ground cardamom

1/2 tsp salt

1 tbsp vegetable oil

1 Chinese duck

banana leaves (enough to wrap duck, about 2 feet)

In food processor, chop nuts, turmeric, galangal, lemongrass, garlic, shallots and chilies until very fine. Add coriander seeds, nutmeg, cinnamon, cloves, cardamom and salt; process until combined. In a nonstick skillet, heat oil over low heat; cook spice mixture until fragrant, 4 to 5 minutes. Let cool.

Wash duck under cold running water. Remove neck and giblets and pat dry inside and out. Using hands and small sharp knife, loosen skin all the way around duck, being careful not to tear it. Spread spice mixture under skin, on top of skin and in cavity of duck.

Wrap duck in banana leaves, then in foil. Bake in 350°F oven for 3 1/2 hours. Carefully remove foil and banana leaves, saving leaves for presentation. Increase temperature to 475°F; cook duck 10 to 12 minutes longer or until skin is brown and crisp. Line serving platter with reserved banana leaves; place duck on top. Serves 2.

Wine suggestion — 2000 Cave Spring Cellars Riesling Indian Summer Select Late Harvest

Mennonite buggy

PORK TENDERLOIN WITH FOUR PEPPERCORN CRUST AND APPLE CALVADOS JUS

THE ELM HURST INN, INGERSOLL, ON / *Executive Chef: Darrell Stewart*

The slight fruity flavour of the sauce offsets the spiciness of the peppercorns in this delightful entrée. The creamy buttered spinach accents the pork nicely.

3 tbsp coarsely crushed peppercorns (pink, green, black and white)

3 pork tenderloins, each 12 oz (tail ends cut off and trimmed)

1/4 cup clarified butter

1/4 cup Calvados or brandy

1/2 cup apple cider

3/4 cup homemade beef jus lié (or Knorr demi-glaze or jus lié)

1/4 cup butter

1 1/2 bags (10 oz) fresh spinach

3 medium portobello mushrooms, cut into quarters

3 tbsp olive oil

1 clove garlic, minced

salt and pepper

Sprinkle crushed peppercorns over 1 side of each tenderloin; press lightly onto pork.

In ovenproof skillet over medium-high heat, heat clarified butter; sear pork, peppercorn side down. Turn over and roast in 400°F oven for about 15 minutes or until juices run clear when pork is pierced and just a hint of pink remains inside. Remove from skillet and keep warm.

Drain fat from pan. Over high heat, deglaze pan with brandy. Add apple cider and jus lié; reduce by one-third.

In separate large skillet, melt butter; add 2 tbsp water. Add spinach; sauté just until wilted. Set aside.

Toss mushrooms with olive oil and garlic; season with salt and pepper to taste. Transfer to barbecue over medium heat or under broiler; grill on both sides.

Slice each pork tenderloin into about 8 slices. Divide spinach among 6 plates. Fan pork slices over top. Spoon sauce over pork and top with mushrooms. Serves 6.

Wine suggestion — 2000 Southbrook Blush

GRILLED PROVIMI VEAL CHOP WITH A FARCE OF VARIOUS MUSHROOMS, SPINACH AND ASIAGO CHEESE

THE WESTOVER INN, ST. MARYS, ON / *Innkeepers: Julie Docker-Johnson and Stephen McCotter*

Serve this great-tasting veal dish with rösti potatoes (recipe follows), roasted baby onions and parsley root.

1/4 cup olive oil

4 large shallots, finely minced

2 cups finely minced mixed mushrooms (portobello, shiitake, oyster, etc.)

1/3 cup cooked, drained chopped fresh or frozen spinach

4 tsp finely minced garlic

2 tbsp bread crumbs

1/2 cup shredded Asiago cheese

salt and pepper

6 Provimi veal chops, each 8 oz

In skillet, heat oil over medium heat; sauté shallots until translucent. Add mushrooms, spinach, garlic and bread crumbs; sauté for 2 minutes. Let cool. Add Asiago cheese. Mix thoroughly; season with salt and pepper to taste.

Make incision about 3/4 inch long and 1 1/2 inches deep on fat side of veal chop near bone. Stuff pocket with mushroom mixture and secure with toothpicks. In skillet, heat oil over high heat; sear veal for about 2 minutes per side. Place on baking sheet and roast in 375°F oven for 10 to 12 minutes.

Wine suggestion — 1999 Inniskillin Cabernet Franc Reserve

6 Yukon Gold potatoes, peeled

salt and pepper

4 tsp unsalted butter

Rösti Potatoes

In food processor, grate potatoes. Squeeze out excess water and season with salt and pepper to taste.

In nonstick skillet over medium-high heat, melt half of the butter. Layer grated potato in skillet and pack down to form 1 large pancake; cook until browned. Place large inverted plate over pancake. Turn over skillet so that pancake is transferred to plate. Add remaining butter to skillet and slide pancake back into skillet; cook until browned. Place on baking sheet and roast in 375°F oven for about 10 minutes or until potatoes are tender. Serve with veal. Serves 6.

GRILLED ONTARIO PORK TENDERLOIN WITH RIESLING CREAM CORN AND ASPARAGUS CRISPIN APPLE FRITTERS

HILLEBRAND ESTATES WINERY RESTAURANT, NIAGARA-ON-THE-LAKE, ON / *Executive Chef: Tony de Luca*

The colourful and fresh Harvest Riesling cream corn and the fritters are a beautiful combination with the pork tenderloin.

2 pork tenderloins, each 1 lb

2 tbsp olive oil

salt, pepper and cayenne pepper

Brush pork with oil. Season with salt, pepper and cayenne to taste. On grill over high heat, cook tenderloins for 8 minutes; turn and grill for about 4 minutes longer or just until hint of pink remains inside. Cut into 1 1/2-inch slices.

Spoon about 1/4 cup of the Harvest Riesling cream corn onto each of 4 warmed plates. Fan 3 slices of pork tenderloin on top of sauce. Arrange 3 fritters attractively around plate. Serves 4.

Chef's tip: The fritter mixture can be made up to 2 hours in advance.

Wine suggestion — 2000 Hillebrand Estates Lakeshore Chardonnay

---

3/4 cups all purpose flour

1/2 cup bread flour

3 tsp baking powder

1 tsp salt

2 large eggs, beaten

2 cups milk

2 tbsp maple syrup

3/4 cup chopped pecans

1/2 Crispin apple, peeled, cored and chopped into 1/4-inch pieces

3 tsp minced fresh ginger root

1/2 cup peeled, chopped (1/2-inch pieces) asparagus

3 cups vegetable oil

Asparagus Crispin Apple Fritters

In bowl, combine all-purpose and bread flours, baking powder, and salt.

In separate bowl, blend together eggs, milk and maple syrup. Stir in pecans, apple, ginger and asparagus.

Stir apple mixture into flour mixture until blended.

In deep saucepan, heat oil over high heat to 350°F; spoon heaping tablespoon of batter into hot oil and cook until golden brown. Remove with slotted spoon and let drain on paper towel. Repeat with remaining batter. Keep warm.

Harvest Riesling Cream Corn

6 ears corn

1 tbsp olive oil

1 shallot, finely diced

1 clove garlic, minced

1/2 sweet red pepper, cut into 1/4-inch pieces

1/2 sweet yellow pepper, cut into 1/4-inch pieces

1/4 cup Hillebrand's Harvest Riesling 1995

1/2 cup 35% cream

salt and pepper

Husk and clean corn. Slice off kernels. In skillet, heat oil over medium-high heat; sauté shallots, garlic, corn and red and yellow peppers for 2 minutes. Add wine and reduce to 1 tablespoon. Blend in cream and salt and pepper to taste. Keep warm.

MEDALLIONS OF LAMB WITH APRICOTS AND PEPPERCORN HONEY GLAZE

THE GLENERIN INN, MISSISSAUGA, ON / *Executive Chef: John Harnett*

Chef Harnett suggests a variation using Ontario maple syrup instead of the honey and fresh apricots instead of the dried.

2 1/2 lb boneless loin of lamb

1 cup all-purpose flour

salt and pepper

6 to 8 tbsp (approx) unsalted butter

4 tsp crushed green peppercorns

1 1/2 cups dry white wine

1 1/2 cups liquid honey

12 dried apricots

fresh mint

Cut lamb into 1 1/2-inch-thick slices. Place medallions between 2 pieces of waxed paper; using meat mallet, flatten to uniform thickness. In bowl, season flour with salt and pepper to taste; dredge medallions in flour mixture.

In large skillet, melt 2 tbsp of the butter over medium-high heat; sauté medallions in batches (adding more butter as necessary) until cooked to desired doneness and lightly browned on both sides. Transfer to serving platter, cover with foil and keep warm in oven.

Drain excess butter from skillet; add peppercorns to skillet; sauté for 1 minute. Add wine, honey and apricots; bring to boil and simmer for 15 to 20 minutes or until apricots are tender and sauce is thickened to consistency of syrup. Spoon apricots and sauce over the lamb medallions. Garnish with mint. Serves 6.

Wine suggestion — 2000 Birchwood Estate Gewürztraminer Riesling

Birchwood Estates Wines

STEAK AU POIVRE

BAILEY'S, GODERICH, ON / *Owner/Chef: Ben Merritt*

This classic steak has always been on Chef Merritt's menu and probably always will be because some things just shouldn't change.

2 tbsp olive oil

4 striploin steaks, each 8 oz

1/4 cup beef or veal stock

1/4 cup 35% cream

salt

chopped fresh parsley

In large skillet, heat oil over medium-high heat; sauté steaks until cooked to desired doneness. Keep warm in oven.

Drain any fat from skillet; add stock and cream and reduce by half. Add green peppercorn butter and reduce until sauce is thick enough to coat back of wooden spoon. Season with salt to taste. Spoon sauce over steaks; garnish with parsley. Serves 4.

Wine suggestion — 1998 Hillebrand Estates Trius Red

1/2 cup butter

2 tbsp brandy

2 tbsp green peppercorns + 1/2 tsp peppercorn brine

1/2 tsp pepper

pinch salt

Green Peppercorn Butter

In food processor or blender, combine butter, brandy, peppercorns, peppercorn brine, pepper and salt.

GRILLED VENISON CHOP WITH WILTED ARUGULA, RADICCHIO, ENDIVE AND WALNUT BREAD

THE PRINCE OF WALES HOTEL, NIAGARA-ON-THE-LAKE, ON / *Executive Chef: Ralf Bretzigheimer*

This creation of Chef Bretzigheimer is truly delicious, with its wonderful gravy for the venison chop, accompanied by the nut-flavoured wilted lettuces.

1 large bunch arugula

2 heads Belgian endive

1 1/2 large heads radicchio

1 cup frozen cranberries

1 cup Merlot

1/2 cup granulated sugar

1 cup glace de viande, or canned beef or veal gravy

salt and pepper

3 medium Yukon Gold potatoes (unpeeled)

4 tbsp olive oil

2 tbsp butter

3 cups walnut bread, cubed (or dark rye bread and 1/4 cup chopped walnuts)

2 tbsp raspberry vinegar

6 venison loin chops, bone in and frenched

Wash and dry arugula, endive and radicchio. Chop into 1/4-inch strips and set aside.

In saucepan over high heat, combine the cranberries, Merlot and sugar. Bring to boil; boil, stirring constantly, until reduced by one-third. Add glace de viande and salt and pepper to taste. Keep warm over low heat.

Scrub potatoes and cut into 1-inch-thick slices. Arrange on small baking sheet and brush with 2 tbsp of the oil. Bake in 300°F oven until tender.

In large skillet, heat butter over medium-high heat; briefly sauté walnut bread. Add arugula, endive, radicchio and raspberry vinegar; cook until greens are slightly wilted.

In separate large skillet, heat remaining oil over high heat; sear venison chops until medium to medium-rare; keep warm. Arrange potatoes on 1 side of each plate, overlapping in fan shape. On other side of each plate, pile greens mixture. Arrange venison, bone up, in centre of plates. Serves 6.

Wine suggestion — 2000 Henry of Pelham Baco Noir Reserve

CHEESE SOUFFLÉ

ENVER'S, MORRISTON, ON

The good thing about this recipe is that most of the ingredients are right in your refrigerator. You can use any assortment of leftover cheeses such as Cheddar and Stilton. Served with a salad and bread, the soufflé makes a nice lunch or light dinner.

2 tbsp butter

2 tbsp cornstarch

1/2 cup milk

1/2 cup 35% cream

1/2 cup assorted grated cheeses

salt and pepper

4 egg yolks

5 egg whites

In small saucepan, melt the butter over medium heat; blend in cornstarch until smooth. Add milk, cream and cheeses. Cook until cheese is melted; season with salt and pepper to taste.

Add egg yolks to cheese mixture; stir until smooth. Beat egg whites until stiff peaks form; carefully fold in cheese mixture.

Pour into greased baking dish. Place baking dish in roasting pan; pour enough water into pan to come halfway up sides of baking dish. Bake in 350°F oven for 25 minutes. Serves 4 to 6.

Wine suggestion — 2000 Cave Spring Cellars Chardonnay Reserve

GRILLED VEGETABLE AND TOFU TORTES

THE WILDFLOWER RESTAURANT, FONTHILL, ON / *Owner/Chef: Wolfgang Sterr*

This entrée is very popular at The Wildflower, especially in the late summer and harvest season, when all the vegetables have the most flavour and local farmers have lots to offer. In the fall, use some butternut squash or even pumpkin.

1 medium green zucchini

1 medium yellow zucchini

1 medium eggplant

4 Roma tomatoes

1 small red onion

2 sweet red peppers

2 sweet green peppers

1/2 cup extra-virgin olive oil

1/2 cup balsamic vinegar

3 tsp chopped fresh cilantro

2 tsp chopped fresh garlic

salt and pepper

1 block (12.4 oz) extra-firm tofu

6 sheets (each 7 inches square) homemade or purchased pasta

2 cups homemade tomato and herb compote (or jar of tomato sauce enriched by adding two chopped Roma tomatoes)

1/2 cup shredded medium Cheddar cheese

1/2 cup shredded mozzarella cheese

baby greens to serve 6

1 cup of "Wildflowers" Fieldberry Vinaigrette (or homemade or purchased raspberry vinaigrette)

Cut green and yellow zucchini, eggplant, tomatoes and onion into 1/4-inch-thick slices. Cut red and green peppers into 1 1/2-inch-wide strips. Whisk together oil, vinegar, cilantro, garlic and salt and pepper to taste. Add vegetables to oil mixture and marinate for 2 hours. Transfer to barbecue grill over medium-high heat; grill until almost cooked. Remove and set aside.

Cut tofu into thin slices. Blanch pasta sheets until almost cooked.

Brush baking sheet with olive oil. On sheet, layer eggplant slice, 1 tsp tomato compote, zucchini, tofu, tomato, onion and peppers, adding more compote after each layer and finishing with pasta sheet. Sprinkle with Cheddar and mozzarella. Bake in 375°F oven for 5 to 8 minutes or until cheese is melted.

Toss greens in vinaigrette and arrange on 6 plates. Heat remaining tomato compote and top greens with 2 tsp each. Place grilled vegetable pasta torte on compote. Serves 6.

Wine suggestion — 2000 Marynissen Estates Pinot Noir Butler's Grant Vineyard

DESSERTS

Dessert! After a family meal, a dessert can be simple: sliced fruit or cookies. But a dinner party calls for something special — an elegant, sweet conclusion to the meal. It's the last thing your guests will have at your home, and you will want them to leave with a wonderful sweet taste in their mouths. A dessert had better be sufficiently decadent and delicious to be worth the calories.

These recipes surely are. Included in this section are innovative ways to serve fresh fruit such as Raspberries with Mango Sorbet from Rundles. There are wonderfully rich selections such as Creamy Lemon Delight with Cointreau Marinated Strawberries from The Little Inn of Bayfield and Crème Brûlée with Toffeed Strawberries from The Church Restaurant.

For those of you with a sweet tooth, this selection of desserts is sure to satisfy.

◀ Brandy and Vanilla Custard Cake on Three-Berry Compote

LEMON AND MASCARPONE MOUSSE IN PHYLLO

WELLINGTON COURT, ST. CATHARINES, ON / *Executive Chef: Erik Peacock*

The contrasting textures of the mousse with the crispness of the phyllo cup make a heavenly dessert.

1/2 cup unsalted butter

1 cup granulated sugar

1/3 cup lemon juice

4 eggs

1 cup 35% cream

1/4 cup mascarpone cheese

In medium saucepan over low heat, melt 1/2 cup of the butter. Stir in sugar and lemon juice; cook, stirring frequently and without boiling, until sugar is dissolved. Remove from heat.

Whisk eggs. Add lemon mixture and stir until well blended and smooth. Return to saucepan and cook over medium heat, stirring constantly, for about 15 minutes or until thick enough to coat back of wooden spoon.

Pass mixture through sieve into stainless steel or glass bowl. Prepare ice water bath in second bowl. Place bowl of lemon custard in ice water bath and let cool completely.

Meanwhile, whisk 3 tbsp of the cream with mascarpone cheese. In separate bowl, whip remaining cream and set aside in refrigerator. Fold mascarpone cheese into chilled custard until incorporated. Fold in whipped cream. Refrigerate for at least 2 hours or overnight. Fill phyllo cups with lemon mascarpone mousse. Serves 8.

Wine suggestion — 2000 Château des Charmes Late Harvest Riesling

1/4 cup unsalted butter

6 sheets phyllo pastry

icing sugar

Phyllo Pastry Cups

Melt butter. Cut 3 sheets phyllo pastry evenly into 4 to make 12 rectangles. Cover with damp towel to prevent drying out.

Arrange 4 single sheets of phyllo on work surface and brush each with butter. Top each with 2 more sheets, brushing each layer with butter. Place in muffin cups or other cup form. Repeat to make 4 more cups. Bake in 350°F oven for 6 minutes or until golden brown. Sprinkle with icing sugar. (Can be stored, uncovered, at room temperature for up to 1 day.)

Chef's tip: Serve phyllo cups alone or with fruit purée for colour on the plate.

CLAFOUTIS

THE OLD PRUNE RESTAURANT, STRATFORD, ON / *Executive Chef: Bryan Steele*

This is one of the most popular desserts on The Old Prune's summer menu. It's a soufflé-like baked dish that combines the contrasting elements of hot and cold, sour and sweet. Quark is a low-fat cheese readily available in most supermarkets.

2 cups Quark, drained and pressed through sieve

1 1/2 tbsp unsalted butter, softened

2 cups icing sugar

4 egg yolks

1/4 cup 35% cream

rind and juice of 1/2 lemon

1/4 cup cornstarch, sifted

4 egg whites

2 tbsp granulated sugar

1 cup fresh berries (raspberries, blackberries, wild blueberries) or pitted cherries

ice cream

In bowl, beat Quark and butter until light and fluffy. Add icing sugar and continue beating until very light. Beat in egg yolks, 1 at a time. Beat in cream, lemon rind and juice and cornstarch just until combined.

Beat egg whites until soft peaks form; fold into Quark mixture. Grease an 8- x 12-inch glass baking dish or individual 4-inch ramekins. Sprinkle lightly with granulated sugar. Spoon in Quark mixture to come two-thirds of the way up dish. Arrange berries on top. Bake in 450°F oven for 25 to 30 minutes or until tester inserted in centre comes out clean. If baking in individual ramekins, bake for 12 to 15 minutes. Serve warm with scoop of ice cream on top. Serves 6 to 8.

Wine suggestion — 2000 Pelee Island Riesling Icewine

Aerial view of the Festival Theatre, Stratford

HAZELNUT CAPPUCCINO TORTE

KETTLE CREEK INN, PORT STANLEY, ON / *Executive Chef: Frank Hubert*

Hazelnut, chocolate and coffee! What a winning combination in this heavenly, creamy dessert.

3/4 cup toasted hazelnuts

5 1/2 oz bittersweet chocolate

2 tsp orange rind

1 tsp lemon rind

6 large eggs, separated

3/4 cup granulated sugar

8 oz mascarpone cheese

3/4 cup 35% cream

1/8 cup coffee liqueur

1/8 cup Frangelico

1 tbsp espresso granules

freshly ground nutmeg

In food processor, chop hazelnuts, chocolate and orange and lemon rind until finely ground. Set aside.

Beat egg yolks with 1/4 cup of the sugar for 5 minutes or until creamy consistency. Fold into hazelnut mixture.

In separate bowl, beat egg whites until frothy. Gradually beat in another 1/4 cup of the sugar until soft peaks form. Beat until stiff peaks form; fold into hazelnut mixture. Spread in greased floured 8-inch springform pan; bake in 350°F oven for 30 minutes. Let cool; unmould.

In bowl, combine mascarpone cheese, cream, remaining sugar, coffee liqueur and Frangelico; beat until smooth and stiff; spread over cake. Just before serving sprinkle with the espresso granules and nutmeg. Serves 10 to 12.

Liqueur suggestion — Frangelico

CREAMY LEMON DELIGHT WITH COINTREAU-MARINATED STRAWBERRIES

THE LITTLE INN OF BAYFIELD, BAYFIELD, ON

This dessert is so simple to prepare, yet the presentation and flavour are out of this world.

3 1/3 cups 35% cream

1 cup granulated sugar + 2 tbsp

1/2 tbsp gelatin

rind of 3 lemons

juice of 4 lemons

1/2 cup Cointreau

36 whole strawberries, washed, dried and stems removed (kept whole)

6 mint bouquets

In saucepan over medium heat, combine cream, 1 cup of the sugar and gelatin; cook without boiling, until gelatin is dissolved. Whisk rind and juice of 3 lemons into warm cream mixture. Pour into 6 martini or dessert glasses; refrigerate for about 4 hours or until set.

Stir together Cointreau, juice of remaining lemon and remaining 2 tbsp sugar. Pour over strawberries. Let marinate until serving.

To serve, place 6 strawberries, pointed end up, on top of set cream. Pour Cointreau marinade over top. Garnish with mint leaves. Serves 6.

Liqueur suggestion — Cointreau

APPLE RAISIN CAKE WITH HOMEMADE MAPLE WALNUT ICE CREAM

1 cup pecan halves

3/4 cup raisins

1/4 cup bourbon

1 cup sifted cake-and-pastry flour

1 cup all-purpose flour

1 1/2 tsp baking soda

1/2 tsp salt

1/2 tsp nutmeg

1/2 tsp cinnamon

1/4 tsp ground cloves

1/8 tsp mace

2 cups granulated sugar

1 cup vegetable oil

2 large eggs

6 large unpeeled Granny Smith apples, cored and cut into 1/4-inch cubes

KEYSTONE ALLEY CAFÉ, STRATFORD, ON/ *Owner/Chef: Sheldon Russell*

Chef Russell also serves this cake with a fudge sauce made by simmering a can of condensed milk in a saucepan of water (enough to cover the can) for 2 hours. Remove can and allow to completely cool before opening. When you open it, there is an instant fudge sauce. If it's too thick, add a little water.

Toast pecans and chop coarsely. In bowl, combine pecans, raisins and bourbon; cover and marinate for at least 2 hours.

Sift together cake-and-pastry flour, all-purpose flour and baking soda. Stir in salt, nutmeg, cinnamon, cloves and mace. In separate bowl, beat sugar with oil until well blended. Beat in eggs, 1 at a time. Fold in dry ingredients. Add pecan mixture; mix until combined. Stir in diced apples and pour into greased 10-inch round cake pan. Bake in 325°F oven for 1 1/2 hours or until tester inserted in centre comes out clean and dry. Let cool. Serve with maple walnut ice cream. Serves 10 to 12.

Wine suggestion — 1999 EastDell Vidal Icewine

7 egg yolks (medium eggs)

1 cup dark maple syrup

2 cups 35% cream, lightly whipped

1/2 cup chopped walnuts

Maple Walnut Ice Cream

Beat egg yolks lightly.

In saucepan, bring maple syrup to boil; continuing to beat, pour over egg yolks. Beat for 15 to 20 minutes or until cooled. Fold in cream.

Freeze in ice cream machine according to manufacturer's directions, adding walnuts when nearly set; transfer to freezer until frozen. (If using a bowl or mould, add walnuts along with cream.

CRÈME BRÛLÉE WITH TOFFEED STRAWBERRIES

THE CHURCH RESTAURANT, STRATFORD, ON

This beautifully rich and creamy dessert continues to be a favourite.

1 vanilla bean, split and seeds scraped out

1/2 cup milk + 2 tbsp

1 3/4 cups 35% cream

6 1/2 tbsp superfine sugar

9 egg yolks

Mix vanilla seeds with 2 tbsp milk to separate. In bowl, mix together cream, 1/2 cup of the milk, sugar, egg yolks, vanilla pod and seeds. Let stand for 1 hour for flavours to infuse; remove pods.

Pour mixture into 6 2-inch ramekins. Set ramekins in roasting pan and fill pan with enough hot water to come two-thirds of the way up sides of ramekins. Cover pan with foil and bake in 250°F oven for about 1 hour or until set, checking periodically to make sure water is not simmering (if it is, reduce heat to 200°F). Remove ramekins from pan and let cool.

Remove brûlées from ramekins up to 1 hour prior to serving by running knife around edge of ramekin, inverting onto centre of plate and shaking until brûlée releases. Place caramel disc on top. Serve with toffeed strawberries alongside. Serves 6.

Chef's tip: Chef Russell pours crème anglaise around the brûlée and makes a design in it using strawberry sauce. He then places the strawberries along 1 side of the sauce.

Wine suggestion — 2000 Reif Estate Special Select Late Harvest Vidal

6 tbsp superfine sugar

Caramel Tops

Place plain round pastry cutter about 1/4 inch larger than ramekins on lightly oiled nonstick baking sheet; sprinkle with 1 tbsp of the sugar to make thin layer the shape of cutter. Remove cutter, being careful to keep shape intact. Repeat to make 5 more sugar shapes.

Bake in 400°F oven for about 10 minutes or until sugar caramelizes to golden brown, being careful not to burn. Let cool. Gently remove from tray with palette knife.

2 1/4 cups granulated sugar

1/4 cup glucose

12 large strawberries

Toffeed Strawberries

Pour sugar into saucepan and slowly pour water into centre of sugar, adding just enough to cover. Bring to boil and skim off white foam. Add glucose and cook, without stirring, over high heat to 305°F on candy thermometer. Remove from heat at about 311°F.

Insert toothpick in each strawberry; holding toothpick, dip each in sugar mixture. Place on a lightly greased nonstick baking sheet or piece of parchment paper.

BRANDY AND VANILLA CUSTARD CAKE ON THREE-BERRY COMPOTE

THE WESTOVER INN, ST. MARYS, ON / *Innkeepers: Julie Docker-Johnson and Stephen McCotter*

The contrasting colours and flavours are wonderful in this custard cake. It has a light, sweet-tart flavour. Preserved fruit with its liquid also goes well with this dessert, as long as it isn't too sweet.

1 1/2 cups 35% cream

1 cup milk

2/3 cup granulated sugar

1/2 vanilla bean, split and seeds scraped out

9 egg yolks, lightly beaten

1/4 cup brandy

1 tsp vanilla extract

Custard

In saucepan, scald cream and milk along with sugar and vanilla bean and seeds. Let cool. Whisk in yolks. Add brandy and vanilla extract. Strain into 7-inch springform pan lined with plastic wrap. Let stand for 5 minutes to let bubbles escape.

Place in large roasting pan; pour enough water into roasting pan to come halfway up side of springform pan. Cover springform pan with foil. Bake in 325°F oven for about 30 minutes or until custard just sets. (Baking time will vary depending on temperature of mixture when it goes in the oven. Watch carefully, as overbaked custard will turn grainy.) Remove springform pan from water bath; let cool. Cover with plastic wrap and refrigerate until well chilled.

To Assemble: Run knife around cake and gently remove from pan. Trim edge to make even.

Gently remove custard from springform pan; remove plastic wrap from sides only. Brush cake with brandy and place over custard. Invert serving platter over cake and turn cake upside down to transfer to plate, custard side up. Remove bottom of springform pan. Trim custard so that edges are flush with cake. Refrigerate.

Slice just before serving. Spoon compote onto plates. Top with cake slice. Serves 10 to 12.

Wine suggestion — Southbrook Framboise D'Or

Cake

3 egg whites

1/4 cup granulated sugar + 1 tbsp

1/2 tsp lemon juice

1/2 tsp vanilla extract

1/4 cup sifted cake-and-pastry flour

pinch salt

brandy

Beat egg whites until soft peaks form; beat in 1/4 cup of the sugar. Add lemon juice and vanilla and continue beating. Sift together flour, remaining 1 tbsp sugar and salt. Sift half of the mixture over egg whites and gently fold in with whisk; sift remaining mixture and gently fold in.

Scrape into 7-inch springform pan and bake in 350°F oven for 20 to 25 minutes or until golden brown and top springs back when touched. Place upside down on rack; let cool completely.

Three-Berry Compote

1 cup each frozen strawberries, raspberries and blueberries

1/2 cup granulated sugar

1/2 cup apple juice

juice of 1 lemon

In heavy saucepan over low heat, combine berries, sugar, apple juice and lemon juice. Heat gently just until liquid is hot and berries are thawed. Refrigerate.

HILLEBRAND ESTATES TRIUS ICEWINE TRUFFLES

HILLEBRAND'S ESTATE WINERY RESTAURANT, NIAGARA-ON-THE-LAKE, ON / *Executive Chef: Tony de Luca*

These truffles surprise with a small burst of icewine when you bite into them.

1 lb semisweet chocolate, chopped

1/4 cup 35% cream

1/4 vanilla bean

2 1/2 tbsp unsalted sweet butter, cut in bits

Hillebrand Estate's Trius Icewine

unsweetened cocoa powder or icing sugar

Place chopped chocolate in stainless steel or glass bowl. In small saucepan over high heat, scald cream and vanilla bean. Remove vanilla bean. Immediately pour cream over chocolate; stir gently until chocolate is melted. Stir in butter in small pieces until melted. Let chocolate cool, cover and refrigerate overnight.

Form balls by rolling about 1 tbsp of the mixture in palm of hand. Place on baking sheet, cover and refrigerate for 45 minutes.

Using index finger, form hollow in each truffle. Using syringe, inject hollow with small amount of icewine. Pinch truffle closed. Cover and refrigerate for 2 hours. Dust with cocoa powder. Makes 35 - 40 truffles.

Wine suggestion — 2002 Hillebrand Estates Trius Icewine

RIESLING-MARINATED BERRIES WITH BREAD AND BUTTER PUDDING

QUEEN'S LANDING INN & CONFERENCE RESORT, NIAGARA-ON-THE-LAKE, ON / *Pastry Chef: Catherine O'Donnell*

Frozen berries work as well as fresh for this recipe according to Chef O'Donnell. The amount of berries may be varied depending on the consistency of sauce you desire.

1/2 bottle Riesling wine

1 1/4 cups icing sugar

1 cup lemon juice

1/3 cup arrowroot or cornstarch

1/2 cup water

1 cup each fresh or frozen blueberries, raspberries and strawberries

In saucepan over medium-high heat, bring wine, icing sugar and lemon juice to a boil. Dissolve arrowroot in water and blend thoroughly; whisk into wine mixture.

Remove from heat and stir in blueberries. Let cool. Stir in raspberries and strawberries.

Spoon bread and butter pudding onto each of 8 plates and spoon Riesling-marinated berries on top. Serves 8.

Wine suggestion — 2000 Birchwood Estates Cabernet Franc Icewine

10 whole eggs

1 cup + 1 tbsp granulated sugar

1/2 tsp nutmeg

1/2 tsp cinnamon

6 1/4 cups milk

1 cup raisins or apples or cranberries

10 croissants (or 11 slices of bread with crust and 4 tbsp butter)

1/4 tsp cinnamon

Bread and Butter Pudding

Whisk eggs with 1 cup sugar until smooth. Whisk in nutmeg and cinnamon. Stir in milk and strain into bowl. Stir in raisins. Soak bread in milk mixture for 3 to 5 minutes.

Transfer soaked bread to ovenproof casserole. Pour remaining milk mixture over bread. Combine remaining sugar with cinnamon and dust over pudding. Set aside. Place casserole in roasting pan; pour enough water into pan to come one-quarter of the way up side of casserole. Bake in 350°F oven for 45 minutes.

RASPBERRIES WITH MANGO SORBET

RUNDLES, STRATFORD, ON / *Executive Chef: Neil Baxter*

This is a delightfully light, colourful dessert full of fresh fruit flavour.

3 pints raspberries

mint leaves

Carefully spoon marinated raspberries into individual serving glasses and spoon in enough of the liquid to come two-thirds of the way up berries. Top with scoop of sorbet and garnish with mint leaves. Serves 6.

Wine suggestion — Southbrook Framboise D'Or

---

3 ripe mangoes (to yield 4 cups pulp)

1 1/2 cups fruity white wine

1 cup simple syrup (see chef's tip)

juice of 1 lemon

Mango Sorbet

Peel mangoes. Remove flesh from stone and purée in food processor or blender until smooth. Add wine, syrup and lemon juice; blend for 5 seconds. Spoon into ice cream maker and freeze according to manufacturer's instructions.

Chef's tip: To make simple syrup, bring 1/2 cup granulated sugar and 1/2 cup water to boil briefly; let cool. The sorbet base can be made several days ahead and stored in refrigerator. Freeze sorbet several hours ahead of time, but not too long, as ice crystals build up and sorbet will not be as smooth.

---

1 cup freshly squeezed orange juice

1/2 cup fruity white wine

2 tbsp granulated sugar

juice of 1/2 lemon

6 mint leaves

Raspberry Marinade

In bowl, stir together orange juice, wine, sugar, lemon juice and mint leaves until sugar is dissolved. Stir in raspberries and let stand for 1 hour.

THYME ICE CREAM

THE OTHER BROTHER'S, GUELPH, ON

The essence of this ice cream is in its subtle but unusually distinct flavour. The delicate infusing of the thyme into the cream is the important step to achieve a fabulous result.

2 cups 35% cream

1/2 cup 10% cream

1/2 bunch fresh thyme

6 large egg yolks

1/2 cup granulated sugar

juice of 2 lemons

In saucepan, stir together 35% cream, 10% cream and thyme; bring to boil. Remove from heat and let steep for about 30 minutes, tasting periodically to monitor strength of infusion.

Strain through fine sieve and discard thyme. Return cream to saucepan and bring to boil again. Let cool slightly.

Lightly beat egg yolks with sugar. Gradually add cream mixture, whisking constantly. Return to medium heat and cook gently until thick enough to coat back of spoon. Whisk in lemon juice and pass through fine sieve again. Let cool for 20 to 30 minutes.

Freeze in ice cream machine following manufacturer's instructions. Transfer to freezer for at least 4 hours before serving. Serves 6.

Chef's tip: During steeping, the flavouring can become overpowering depending on the size, strength and variety of thyme. Taste periodically to monitor. Taste should be subtle but recognizable.

Wine suggestion — 1998 Hillebrand Estates Riesling Icewine

BREADS & BREAKFAST FOODS

There is nothing like the aroma of freshly baked bread to bring the whole family into the kitchen.

The Brown, and Muesli Breads from Village Harvest or the Smoked Bacon Corn Bread with Root Cellar Vegetable Slather from The Pillar and Post Inn are delicious, savory, comfort breads — great served on their own or with a soup, stew or pot of beans. The Sunrise or Scrumptious Egg Casseroles from the Stone Maiden Inn are quick and easy to prepare and would make a special breakfast for family and friends. The Decadent French Toast from the Stone Maiden Inn or Scones with Clotted Cream from Lakewinds Country Manor would make lovely brunches or special occasion breakfasts on Christmas morning or Mother's or Father's Day.

◀ Decadent French Toast

DECADENT FRENCH TOAST

STONE MAIDEN INN, STRATFORD, ON / *Innkeepers: Elaine and Jim Spencer*

The name of this dish says it all! It makes a lovely Christmas morning breakfast or brunch. You can substitute almost any fruit for the bananas, including small blueberries or peaches. Raisin, egg and homemade breads are also ideal. Prepare the dish the night before, ready to bake in the morning.

2 tbsp corn syrup (preferably dark)

1 cup brown sugar

5 tbsp margarine or butter

16 (approx) slices whole wheat bread, crusts removed

3 or 4 ripe bananas

5 large eggs

1 1/2 cups milk

1 tsp vanilla

1 tbsp cinnamon

1/2 cup sour cream

1 1/2 cups fresh strawberries, hulled (or 1 pkg., 10 oz, frozen unsweetened berries, partially thawed)

In heavy saucepan, combine corn syrup, brown sugar and margarine; cook, stirring constantly, until bubbly.

Pour corn syrup mixture into greased 13- x 9-inch glass baking dish. Nestle half of the bread slices into syrup, trimming to fit corners and edges. Slice bananas and spread over bread. Cover with remaining bread.

Whisk together eggs, milk and vanilla; pour over bread, coating well. Sprinkle with cinnamon. (Can be covered with plastic wrap and refrigerated overnight.)

Bake in 350°F oven for 45 minutes. To serve, loosen edges of bread from dish with knife. Invert serving platter on top and quickly turn baking dish upside down so French toast transfers to platter, caramel side up. Top each serving with 1 tbsp of sour cream and some of the berries. Serves 10 to 12.

SCONES WITH NIAGARA-ON-THE-LAKE CLOTTED CREAM

LAKEWINDS, NIAGARA-ON-THE-LAKE, ON / *Owner/Chef: Jane Locke*

While Devon cream is available at some specialty shops, it is often costly. This Canadian adaptation is very good. Serve the scones either fresh from the oven or at room temperature with the clotted cream and your favourite jam.

2 cups all-purpose flour

1 tsp cream of tartar

1/2 tsp baking soda

pinch salt

3 tbsp margarine

4 tbsp (approx) milk

In large bowl, sift together flour, cream of tartar, baking soda and salt. Cut margarine into small pieces and rub into flour with fingertips. Stir 4 tbsp of milk with 4 tbsp of water; pour into flour mixture, mixing with round-bladed knife to make a soft, manageable dough.

Knead dough quickly on lightly floured surface to remove all cracks. Roll dough out to 1/2-inch thickness; cut out 2-inch rounds using plain or fluted pastry cutter. Knead trimmings together, roll out and cut out more scones. Transfer to heated, ungreased baking sheet; brush with milk. Bake near top of 450°F oven for about 10 minutes until well risen and light golden. Serve with clotted cream. Makes 10 to 12 scones.

1/3 cup milk

1 tsp rose water or vanilla

2 blades mace (or 1/4 tsp ground)

1 egg, beaten

1 1/4 cups 35% cream

Clotted Cream

In saucepan over low heat, simmer milk, rose water and mace for 5 minutes. Strain milk mixture into beaten egg, then strain whole mixture into cream. Pour into top of double boiler set over simmering water; bring to 165°F. Pour into dish; let cool, cover and refrigerate undisturbed for 24 hours

SCRUMPTIOUS EGG CASSEROLE

STONE MAIDEN INN, STRATFORD, ON / *Innkeepers: Elaine and Jim Spencer*

This scrumptious egg casserole can be made the night before and popped into the oven in the morning.

1 1/2 lb shredded Cheddar cheese

1/4 cup butter or margarine

1 can (8 oz) mushrooms, chopped or sliced

1/2 medium onion, chopped

1 cup cubed ham (or crisp bacon)

8 eggs

1 3/4 cups milk

1/2 cup all-purpose flour

1 tsp dried parsley

1 tsp salt

Spread half of the cheese in greased 13- x 9-inch glass baking dish. In saucepan, heat butter over medium heat; sauté mushrooms and onions until tender. Let cool. Spread mushroom mixture over cheese. Top with ham and remaining cheese.

Whisk together eggs, milk, flour, parsley and salt; pour over cheese. Bake in 375°F oven for 60 minutes. Serves 10 to 12.

Scrumptious Egg Casserole ▶

---

1 cup diced bacon or ham

12 large eggs

1 tbsp milk

1 tbsp margarine or butter

1 cup sour cream

1 cup shredded Cheddar cheese or mixture of shredded cheeses

SUNRISE CASSEROLE

STONE MAIDEN INN, STRATFORD, ON / *Innkeepers: Elaine and Jim Spencer*

This variation on the popular morning scramble is simple and quick to prepare and tastes great.

In skillet, fry bacon. Whisk eggs with milk. In separate skillet heat margarine over medium-high heat, scramble eggs just until soft.

Spread egg mixture in greased 13- x 9-inch glass baking dish. Spread sour cream over top. Sprinkle with bacon and top with cheese. Bake in 350°F oven for 20 minutes. Serves 6 to 8.

COUNTRY APPLE AND APRICOT MUFFINS

QUEEN'S LANDING INN & CONFERENCE RESORT, NIAGARA-ON-THE-LAKE, ON / *Pastry Chef: Catherine O'Donnell*

Chef O'Donnell recommends Mutsu or Northern Spy apples for these delightful muffins, but any kind will do. She also suggests refrigerating the batter for one day before baking.

3 cups granulated sugar

2 cups milk

1 1/2 cups vegetable oil

3 eggs

1 1/4 cups chopped dried apricots

1/2 cup chopped peeled apples

1 tbsp vanilla

4 cups all-purpose flour

2 cups whole wheat flour

2 cups sour cream

1 1/2 tbsp baking powder

1 tbsp baking soda

In bowl, beat together sugar, milk, oil, eggs, apricots, apples and vanilla until well mixed.

In separate bowl, stir together all-purpose and whole wheat flours, sour cream, baking powder and baking soda. Stir into fruit mixture just until combined (do not overmix). Spoon into greased or paper-lined muffin cups, filling three-quarters full. Bake in 375°F oven for 30 to 35 minutes. Makes 36 muffins.

The Commons, Niagara-on-the-Lake

SMOKED BACON CORN BREAD WITH ROOT CELLAR VEGETABLE SLATHER

THE PILLAR AND POST INN, NIAGARA-ON-THE-LAKE, ON / *Executive Chef: Virginia Marr*

This superb bread, served with the vegetable slather, is a terrific accompaniment to a hearty winter stew or soup. Chef Marr serves the vegetable slather hot or cold. The chicken broth used to cook the vegetables can be saved to make soup.

1 cup (approx) cornmeal

1/2 cup all-purpose flour

1 cup diced cooked smoked bacon

1/4 cup chopped fresh parsley

2 tsp baking powder

1 tsp salt

1/2 tsp baking soda

3/4 tsp cayenne pepper

1 1/4 cups buttermilk

2 large eggs

1/4 cup olive oil

1 cup freshly grated Parmesan cheese

Lightly grease loaf pan and sprinkle liberally with cornmeal to coat sides and bottom.

In bowl, combine 1 cup cornmeal, flour, bacon, parsley, baking powder, salt, baking soda and cayenne.

In small bowl, stir together buttermilk, eggs and oil. Add to flour mixture and stir just until blended. Stir in Parmesan cheese.

Pour batter into prepared loaf pan and bake in 350°F oven for 40 to 45 minutes or until tester inserted in centre comes out clean.

1 small rutabaga, peeled and diced

2 parsnips, peeled and diced

2 carrots, peeled and sliced

1 Yukon Gold potato, peeled and diced

chicken broth

2 tbsp unsalted butter

2 tsp rosemary oil

salt and pepper

Root Cellar Vegetable Slather

In saucepan over medium-high heat, combine rutabaga, parsnips, carrots and potatoes; pour in enough chicken broth to cover. Bring to boil. Cook, uncovered, until fork tender. Strain and mash with potato masher. When smooth, stir in butter, rosemary oil and salt and pepper to taste. Place in crock or ramekins and serve with cornbread. Makes about 3 to 4 cups.

ADELAIDE'S NOVA SCOTIA BROWN BREAD

IDLEWYLD INN, LONDON, ON / *Baker: Doug Huskilson*

The baker's great-grandmother made this bread for her turn-of-the-century family. Her granddaughter, Adelaide, often made it for her children's return from a day at the neighbourhood rink. Serve it with a winter stew or big pot of baked beans.

1 cup quick-cooking rolled oats (not instant)

2 1/2 to 3 cups warm water

1 pkg active dry yeast

2 cups whole wheat flour

2 cups all-purpose flour

1/3 cup blackstrap molasses (or 1/2 cup light molasses)

1 tbsp salt

1 tbsp brown sugar

1 tbsp canola or vegetable oil

butter

Soak rolled oats in 1/2 cup of the water for 30 minutes. Dissolve yeast according to package instructions. Gradually mix together oats, yeast, whole wheat and all-purpose flours, molasses, salt, sugar and oil, slowly adding 2 cups of the water and thoroughly mixing. If dough is stiff, add remaining 1/2 cup water. Knead intensely for 8 to 10 minutes. Dust lightly with flour. Transfer to bowl and cover with plastic wrap. Let stand in a warm place for about 1 hour or until doubled in size.

Punch down dough and form into 4 balls. Place 2 in 1 5- x 9-inch large loaf pan. In second loaf pan, place other 2 balls. Brush lightly with oil. Cover with large mixing bowl, being careful not to let it touch rising dough; let stand in warm place for about 15 minutes or until imprint remains in dough after touching lightly. Bake in 350°F oven for about 40 minutes.

Once baked, pull two loaves apart. Brush with butter and serve warm. Makes 4 loaves.

Chef's tip: Because bread is so dense, you may want to rotate the pans in oven every 15 minutes to ensure uniformity.

MUESLI BREAD

IDLEWYLD INN, LONDON, ON / *Baker: Doug Huskilson*

The Idlewyld Inn's freshly baked breads are supplied by a small local bakery called Village Harvest. This is one of those breads with something for everyone — cereals, fruits and nuts. It's a nutritious bread for people on the run.

1 cup muesli

2 1/2 to 3 cups water at room temperature

1 pkg active dry yeast

2 1/2 cups all-purpose flour

2 1/2 cups whole wheat flour

1 cup shelled sunflower seeds

1 tbsp brown sugar

1 tbsp canola or vegetable oil

1 tbsp salt

1 tsp cinnamon

Soak muesli in 1/2 cup of the water for 1 hour. Dissolve yeast according to package instructions. Gradually mix together muesli mixture, yeast, all-purpose and whole wheat flours, sunflower seeds, sugar, oil, salt and cinnamon, slowly adding 2 cups of the water and thoroughly mixing. If dough is stiff, add remaining 1/2 cup water. Knead aggressively for 5 minutes. Form into ball and dust lightly with flour. Transfer to bowl and cover with plastic wrap. Let rise in warm place for about 1 hour or until doubled in size.

Shape into 3 cylinders and place in large 5- x 9-inch loaf pans. Cover and let rise for another 30 minutes or until imprint remains in dough after touching lightly.

Bake in 375°F oven for about 40 minutes or until bottoms sound hollow when tapped. Remove from pans and let cool on racks. Makes 3 loaves.

Springbank Park, London

PROFILES

THE BENCH BISTRO AT EASTDELL ESTATES WINERY

The view from The Bench Bistro is incredible. From its location on the crest of the Niagara Escarpment, diners are treated to a stunning panorama of the rolling vineyards of Niagara's wine country with the Toronto skyline across the lake. The property is beautifully enhanced by nature trails, perfect for a before or after dinner stroll.

The interior is rustic wood and stone with a large fireplace for cozy dining in winter, and a patio deck for alfresco dining in summer. Besides a broad dining menu, The Bench Bistro offers a very popular Sunday brunch with omelets made to order, plus fruits, meats, sweet rolls and pastries. On Thursdays they "tapas the night away" with seasonally inspired mini plates paired with corresponding wines.

The menu changes seasonally but there are specialties such as lavender-crusted grilled lamb paired with EastDell's own rosè or maple-cured salmon and a glass of crisp 2002 EastDell Estates Riesling that is only available at the winery.

4041 Locust Lane, Beamsville, ON, L0R 1B2
Tel: (905) 563-9463 • Fax: (905) 563-1241 • E-mail: winery@eastdell.com
Web site: www.eastdell.com • Open year-round • Lunch and dinner: daily Easter through to the Sunday after New Year's • Winter Hours: Lunch and dinner: Wednesday through Saturday • Sunday: brunch only • Innkeepers: Susan O'Dell and Michael East

BAILEY'S RESTAURANT

Bailey's Restaurant is located on the square in picturesque downtown Goderich. Dine amongst beautiful antiques in a cozy atmosphere. Share a moment on their outdoor patio before walking minutes away to watch one of Goderich's famous sunsets.

The eclectic cuisine at Bailey's is changed regularly, boasting lunch specialties such as baked goat's cheese wrapped in phyllo pastry or Thai shrimp. The saffron-scented seafood chowder is particularly delicious. Dinner specialties include fresh lake fish, roast duck and roast rack of lamb.

120 The Courthouse Square, Goderich, ON, N7A 1M8
Telephone: (519) 524-5166 • Open year-round • Closed Sunday • Lunch and Dinner: Tuesday through Saturday • Lunch only: Monday • Restaurateurs: Ben and Carolyn Merritt

BENMILLER INN & SPA

Housed in five strikingly restored pioneer mills and mill owners' homes, the Benmiller Inn offers fifty-nine guest rooms carefully furnished with comfort in mind. Many rooms have balconies overlooking the Maitland River. The inn's amenities include a fitness area with indoor pool, whirlpool and sauna, a games room with billiards and darts and full spa services.

The Benmiller's Ivey Dining Room, open to inn guests and walk-in diners for breakfast, lunch and dinner, is perched over the tumbling waters of Sharpe's Creek. Local Huron County products such as beef, trout, rabbit, maple syrup and berries are key ingredients on the menu.

Chef John Kloss' emphasis is on presenting light, naturally flavoured cuisine.

RR #4, Goderich, ON, N7A 3Y1
Telephone: (519) 524-2191 or 1-800-265-1711 • Fax: (519) 524-5150
E-mail: info@benmiller.on.ca • Web site: www.benmiller.on.ca •
Open year-round • Innkeeper: Pierre Bergeron

BHIMA'S WARUNG INTERNATIONAL

The restaurant's name derives from "Bhima," a god in the famous Hindu epic "The Mahabarahta," who had a special talent for cooking and hosting large gatherings and whose name, coincidentally, is similar to that of chef/owner Paul Boehmer. Paul was born locally, but spent many years traveling and apprenticing in the techniques of classic and modern cookery in Canada, the United States, Europe and Asia. He acquired ancient recipes from an interesting variety of relatives from Afghanistan to Sri Lanka to Vietnam.

Located in a two-storey office building, this sixty-seat restaurant looks unassuming, but in fact conceals another world of sights, smells and tastes. For alfresco dining they have a lovely garden with Brussels stone and a soothing fishpond. Beginning with classic South East Asian recipes, Bhima's makes them unique by marrying French techniques with Canadian ingredients, such as wild caribou and local rack of lamb. The seasonal specials include exotic tropical fish and the menu is complemented by a large selection of privately stocked Asian beers and exotic fruit drinks. They also have an extensive wine list with all wines by the glass. Terrific!

262 King Street North, Waterloo, ON, N2J 2Y9
Telephone: (519) 747-0722 • Fax: (519) 747-0071 •
E-mail: bhimaswarung@hotmail.com • Open year-round • Dinner: open nightly
Restaurateurs: Paul Boehmer and Nicole Helbig

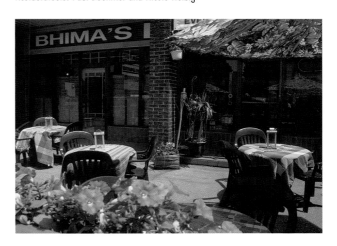

BLACKSHOP RESTAURANT & LOUNGE

The Blackshop Restaurant got its name from its previous location decorated to resemble a European blacksmith shop. Today, it is housed in an elegant stone building in historic downtown Galt. The main dining room seats sixty-five and is complemented by a fireplace lounge with a lovely cherry-wood bar. There is also a large private room for cocktail parties, weddings, seminars, or special functions.

The Blackshop features casual dining with European flair. Continental cuisine is its specialty, but the kitchen produces everything from calamari, to lamb, to fresh fish and great pastas.

20 Hobson Street, Cambridge, ON, N1S 2M6
Telephone: (519) 621-4180 • Fax: (519) 621-9128 • Open year-round • Dinner: open daily • Lunch: Monday through Saturday • Open Sunday for dinner • Restaurateurs: The Cerny Family

CASA MIA RISTORANTE & BAR

This is one of Niagara Falls' most delightful Italian cuisine dining experiences. The Mollica family, mother Lucy with son Claudio, are in charge of the kitchen, both making mouth-watering dishes, with brother Dominic taking care of the front of house.

The elegant dining rooms are contemporary Italian (not a checkered table cloth in sight) divided by statuesque pillars and accented with dramatic flower arrangements. Their signature dishes are Provimi veal, steaks and lobster with fresh-made pastas such as gnocchi Gorgonzola, cannelloni Fiorentina, duck linguini, or simply fettuccine with fresh tomato and basil.

The wine list is wonderfully designed by progressively grouping wines according to weight — light, medium and full bodied. Within each category are wines from all over the world. In addition to their regular list they have a

"Proprietor's Cellar Wine List" of special wines from fine vintages and producers, all available in regular, large or small bottles. On Fridays and Saturdays there is live entertainment from 10 pm to midnight with complimentary taxi service, within city limits, to and from the restaurant.

3518 Portage Road, Niagara Falls, ON, L2J 2K4
Telephone: (905) 356-5410 • Fax: (905) 356-5419 •
E-mail: dominic@casamiaristorante.com • Web site: www.casamiaristorante.com
Open year-round • Lunch: Monday through Friday • Dinner: Monday through Sunday • Restaurateurs: The Mollica Family

THE CHURCH RESTAURANT

The Church Restaurant is located near the Avon Theatre in downtown Stratford. It is housed in a historic building that dates back more than a century, when, in 1874, the congregation held its first service. Dwindling membership took its toll over the years and in 1975 the building was purchased and reopened as The Church Restaurant.

Diners enjoy the original architecture; stained glass windows, organ pipes and a gracious atmosphere that equals the fine food and thoughtful service. The menu, innovatively French, also reflects executive chef Amede Lamarche's interest in global foods.

70 Brunswick Street, Stratford, ON, N5A 3M1
Telephone: (519) 273-3424 • Fax: (519) 272-0061 •
E-mail: mark.craft@churchrestaurant.ca • Web site: www.churchrestaurant.ca
Open: May 6 to December 25 • Closed: Monday • Lunch and Dinner: Tuesday through Sunday • Restaurateur: Mark Craft

DEVLIN'S COUNTRY BISTRO & CATERING

Beginning in 1884, five generations of Devlins operated Mount Pleasant's General Store and Post Office. When it closed in 1990, Chris Devlin transformed the old store into a restaurant. Devlin's is now a pretty, white-framed building situated in Mount Pleasant, a small Ontario town in the countryside south of Brantford. The interior is relaxed yet elegant and features original art by local artists.

Devlin's delicious contemporary Italian cuisine uses today's modern flavours and products and makes use of seasonal local products when available. Diners will enjoy specialties such as Latka with shitake, grilled scallop and flying fish caviar, salmon carpaccio with Champagne vinaigrette, veal scaloppini with oyster mushroom gnocchi, Dover sole stuffed with smoked salmon and grilled scallops or pan roasted quails with vegetable stew and dumplings. Bread is baked in the kitchen every morning.

704 Mount Pleasant Road, Mount Pleasant, ON, N0E 1K0
Telephone: (519) 484-2258 • Fax: (519) 484-2037 •
E-mail: devlins@kwic.com • Web site: www.devlinscountrybistro.com •
Open year-round • Closed Sunday • Dinner: Monday through Saturday •
Lunch: Friday • Restaurateur: Chris Devlin

EDGEWATER MANOR RESTAURANT

Edgewater Manor Restaurant is located on the shores of Lake Ontario in an elegant 1920s mansion. The materials from which it was made were sourced from all over the world by Phillip Morris, a prominent lawyer of the times. In the foyer, for instance, is an imposing marble staircase that was once the centrepiece of the old Toronto Dominion Centre in Toronto.

The manor was the Morris family's private home until 1996 when partners Alex Trajkovski and Terry Terpoy bought it from the family and opened it as a fine dining spot which now attracts guests from across the U.S. and Canada. The menu is "eclectic continental." On the one hand, you can find such popular items as rack of lamb served in a Gewürztraminer crème anglaise or a New York black angus steak with a red wine reduction; on the other hand, you can find exotic dishes such as wild musk ox from Banks Island north of the Arctic Circle, or oven-roasted bison filet, caribou hind medallions or pheasant breast.

Regional wines of the world complement the menu, plus they have a special vintage selections wine list on request.

518 Fruitland Road Stoney Creek, ON, L8E 5A6
Telephone: (905) 643-9332 • Fax: (905) 643-8477 •
Web site: www.edgewatermanor.com • Open year-round • Closed Sunday and public holidays • Lunch and Dinner: Monday through Friday •
Dinner only: Saturday • Restaurateurs: Alex Trajkovski and Terry Terpoy

ELM HURST INN

This Victorian Gothic home was built in 1872 as a residence for James Harris, a prominent fruit and dairy merchant. Today, the inn's forty-nine individually decorated rooms and suites have a subtle blend of country charm and modern amenities. Some of the activities available to visitors include swimming, ice skating, badminton and billiards. Additional facilities include a fitness centre, hiking trails and spa.

The Elm Hurst's dining room is very gracious and offers a monthly schedule of theme dinners, such as Greek or Asian nights and Sunday evening roast beef dinners. The inn's well-known Sunday brunch includes a seafood and salad table, freshly carved roasts and dozens of choices of sweets. The buffet is accompanied by live music, usually violin or classical guitar. Off-site guests are welcome.

415 Harris Street, Ingersoll, ON, N5C 3J8
Telephone: (519) 485-5321 or 1-800-561-5321 • Fax: (519) 485-6579
Open year-round • Lunch and Dinner: daily • Sunday brunch •
Innkeeper: Pat Davies

ELORA MILL INN

The Elora Mill, a 150-year-old grist mill turned country inn, has a dramatic setting, towering above the thundering falls of the Grand River. There are thirty-two uniquely designed rooms and suites divided among four historic buildings in the heart of Ontario's festival country.

The Mill's fireside dining room overlooks the roaring falls. The menu is based around a cornucopia of local foods — trout, apples, cheeses, maple syrup, lamb and organically grown produce — and is complemented by an excellent wine list praised for its wide range of Ontario wines. The Innkeeper's Breakfast, which is included with an overnight stay, features granola and preserves.

77 Mill Street West, Elora, ON, N0B 1S0
Telephone: (519) 846-9118 • Fax: (519) 846-9180 • Open year-round
Lunch and Dinner: daily • Innkeeper: Jennifer Smith

ENVER'S RESTAURANT

Enver's is housed in a heritage building in the hamlet of Morriston, a short drive from Guelph or Hamilton. An intimate fine dining restaurant with eclectic continental cuisine using Asian and new world spicing, Enver's is noted for its extensive wine list. It features a good representation from Niagara and notable vineyards worldwide. There are wine tasting dinners featured throughout the year, pairing wines with innovative cuisine.

42 Queen Street, Morriston, ON, N0B 2C0
Telephone: (519) 821-2852 • Fax: (519) 763-9279 • Open year-round
Closed Sunday and Monday • Lunch: Wednesday through Friday
Dinner: Tuesday through Saturday • Restaurateurs: John and Terri Manolis

THE EPICUREAN

Located on the main street of historic Niagara-on-the-Lake, The Epicurean serves made-to-order gourmet sandwiches, salads, home-made soups, light meals and scrumptious desserts. The Epicurean has become a favourite lunchtime spot in the renowned theatre town.

In the evening, The Grill at The Epicurean serves a

sophisticated bistro menu. Chef John Woods presents elegant, accessible dishes, designed to harmonize with a carefully selected wine list showcasing the finest VQA wines from the Niagara region.

The Epicurean offers a casually sophisticated dining room with a Provençal flair. Terra cotta floors and rich umber walls are complemented by a flower-encircled front patio from which guests can enjoy people watching on Queen Street.

The real jewel is the "secret" patio in the back, a tree-shaded oasis secluded from the main street. Under bistro umbrellas and surrounded by gorgeous gardens, guests can experience all The Epicurean has to offer: gourmet lunches, pre-theatre dinner with swift yet friendly service or lingering over a leisurely meal as the sun sets, candles are lit and the patio lights are turned on. It's a special place that has made its mark in Niagara.

84 Queen Street, Niagara-on-the-Lake, ON, L0S 1J0
Telephone: (905) 468-3408 • Web site: www.epicurean.ca
Open year-round for lunch and dinner • Take out available • Fully accessible
Restaurateurs: Scott and Ruth Aspinall

GLENERIN INN

Glenerin Inn was originally built in 1927 for William Watson Evans, a wealthy Toronto businessman, as a summer retreat for his family. Rescued from demolition in 1984, the Glenerin now stands proudly as one of Mississauga's most elegant and architecturally significant historic sites.

A blend of old world charm and modern amenities, The Glenerin houses a lobby that is grand, yet warm and cozy. There are thirty-nine guest rooms and suites, each uniquely furnished with period antiques and reproductions. Fireplaces and private whirlpool baths are found in some suites, and the inn offers conference rooms in a variety of sizes.

Breakfast, lunch and dinner are served in the inn's restaurant, Thatcher's, for inn guests and walk-in diners. In the warmer months, guests enjoy dining on the covered patio garden overlooking the Sawmill Valley Conservation Area and its beautiful wooded walking trails.

1695 The Collegeway, Mississauga, ON, L5L 3S7
Telephone/fax: (905) 828-6103 • Reservations: (905) 829-7449 or 1-800-267-0525 • Open year-round • Innkeeper: Geoff Slater

HILLEBRAND ESTATES WINERY RESTAURANT

Hillebrand Estates Winery is located at the centre of Niagara's wine country, but visitors are free to do much more than just taste wines. A winery tour including a tutored tasting of Hillebrand's latest VQA wines is one way to enjoy the property. Guests can also browse the rare vintages in the Wine Boutique, take a vineyard bicycle tour or attend one of the winery's many special events.

Hillebrand Estates Winery Restaurant is built into the very heart of the winery, overlooking the barrel cellar and the vineyards. Its wall of windows creates a very open and airy feeling and offers a spectacular view of the Niagara Escarpment. Chef Antonio de Luca's approach to wine country cuisine utilizes fresh seasonal ingredients from the area. His philosophy is to accent the true flavours of foods and to marry suitable combinations.

1249 Niagara Stone Road, Niagara-on-the-Lake, ON, L0S 1J0
Telephone: (905) 468-7123 • Fax: (905) 468-4789 •
Web site: www.hillebrand.com • Open year-round • Winemaker: J-L Groux
Chef: Antonio de Luca

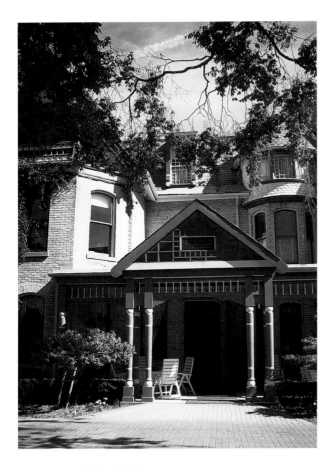

INN ON THE TWENTY

Inn on the Twenty is located in the town of Jordan in a renovated sugar warehouse that dates back to Niagara's earliest years as a wine growing region. The decor is luxurious with stone hearths and counters, classic columns and refined colour schemes. There are sixteen elegant suites, half of them two-storey. The bi-level suites feature a living room, fireplace and powder room on the lower level, and a bedroom and full bath with whirlpool on the upper level. A full service spa is also part of the inn's offerings with a range of relaxation treatments.

All guests are welcome to a winery tour and tasting at Cave Spring Cellars, located across the street from the inn. The quaint little village has a number of shops with unique products, including three antique stores. Cave Spring Cellars has a store offering fine wines and accessories.

Across the road from the inn is the inn's restaurant, On The Twenty. The restaurant has the feel of old Europe with warmth and elegance. It has beautiful stone and iron work and large displays of fresh herbs. Chef Rob Fracchioni is committed to using fresh, locally grown ingredients to develop a unique Niagara style of cooking that is superb.

3845 Main Street, Jordan, ON, L0R 1S0
Telephone: (905) 562-5336 or 1-800-701-8074 • Fax: (905) 562-3232 •
E-mail: vintners@niagara.net • Open year-round • private events •
Innkeeper: Helen Young

IDLEWYLD INN

Idlewyld Inn was built in 1878 as a residence for Charles S. Hyman, a wealthy London businessman, sportsman and politician. Today, this bed-and-breakfast is situated in a residential London neighbourhood, minutes from downtown shops, theatres and restaurants. The decor is elegant and charming. Ornate wood mouldings, intricately carved fireplaces and a massive central staircase have all been meticulously restored. Each of the twenty-seven guest rooms boasts its own unique decor — a subtle blending of antique furnishings and modern amenities — and some contain whirlpools. The inn's gracious living room invites guests to relax by the fireplace and be swept away by the surroundings. Each morning a light breakfast is served in the lovely breakfast room or on the garden patio.

Idlewyld Inn has private facilities to accommodate up to sixty people for catered business meetings, social functions, or weddings.

36 Grand Avenue, London, ON, N6C 1K8
Telephone/fax: (519) 433-2891 • Open year-round •
Innkeeper: Christine Kohl

JANET LYNN'S BISTRO

Janet and Kevin are the husband and wife team of Janet Lynn's Bistro in uptown Waterloo. Janet is the chef and Kevin is the restaurant manager and sommelier.

The restaurant is casually elegant and beautifully designed with four English garden murals painted by renowned local artist, Peter Etril Snyder.

The cuisine is fresh market with French and Italian influences. The delicious and wonderfully presented menu selections are changed seasonally and may include corn-fed chicken stuffed with organic spinach, mascarpone cheese with fettuccine and morels, and grilled lamb tenderloin with feta cheese, onion confit, kalamata olives and warm marinated beets. The wine list hosts a selection of over 100 vintage wines and reserve (rare) wines on request.

92 King Street South, Waterloo, ON, N2J 1P5
Telephone: (519) 725-3440 • Fax: (519) 725-5580 • Open year-round •
Closed Sunday and Monday; Lunch and Dinner: Tuesday through Friday. •
Restaurateur: Janet Leslie and Kevin Wong

KETTLE CREEK INN

Kettle Creek Inn is nestled in the heart of Port Stanley's small fishing village on Lake Erie's north shore. The inn, built in 1849, consists of five luxury suites with whirlpools, baths, gas fireplaces, living rooms and private balconies, as well as ten unique guest rooms with private baths. Guests can relax by the fire in the cozy parlour, have a drink in the pub or dine in the relaxed European bistro atmosphere of one of three dining rooms. During fair weather, gazebo and patio tables are also available. Off-site guests are welcome for lunch and dinner.

Chef Frank Hubert creates such fresh market dinner specialties as locally raised rhea (similar to an ostrich, though slightly smaller), fresh perch, pickerel, trout and Brome Lake duck.

The community offers such activities as sailing and fishing charters, two sandy beaches, summer theatre, tours of the historic Port Stanley Terminal Railway, golf courses, hiking and bird-watching.

216 Joseph Street, Port Stanley, ON, N5L 1C4
Telephone: (519) 782-3388 • Fax: (519) 782-4747 •
E-mail: kci@webgate.net • Open year-round • Lunch and Dinner: daily •
Innkeepers: Jean Strickland and Gary Vedova

KEYSTONE ALLEY CAFÉ

"The Keystone," as the locals fondly refer to it, is located near Stratford's Avon Theatre and unique shops.

A café by day; a dining experience by night is an apt description for this popular restaurant. The luncheon menu offers homemade soups, salads, pastas and sandwiches. The dinner menu, with a French influence, pays close attention to fresh ingredients and presentation. The desserts are delectable. With an open kitchen concept, the Keystone has an atmosphere that is relaxed and its service is attentive.

Under the watchful eye of executive chef and co-owner Sheldon Russell, the twenty-year-old restaurant has become a favourite with locals and visitors alike.

34 Brunswick Street, Stratford, ON, N5A 3L8
Telephone: (519) 271-5645 • Open year-round • Closed Sunday and Monday •
Lunch: Tuesday through Saturday • Dinner: Tuesday through Saturday •
Chef/proprietor: Sheldon Russell

THE KIELY INN AND RESTAURANT

The Kiely Inn was built in 1832 as a family home by Charles Richardson. It is a superb example of post and beam construction and there are many features of historical and architectural interest, which are protected by a historic designation. This magnificent late-Georgian house has twelve guest rooms decorated in the style of the period with antiques and delicately coloured wallpaper. Half of the rooms have wood-burning fireplaces. The Kiely Inn is situated on Niagara-on-the-Lake's main street on one acre of lawns and gardens, overlooking a golf course and Lake Ontario. It is within walking distance to the Shaw Theatre and shops.

The dining room is housed in two rooms, both of which have a formal, elegant ambiance with large wood-burning fireplaces and fine mirrors gracing their mantels. The dining rooms are almost unchanged from their original state, and the central gaseliers, suspended staircase and curved door are all of interest. The cuisine is Continental with a Mediterranean flair, using fresh Niagara ingredients.

209 Queen Street, Niagara-on-the-Lake, ON, L0S 1J0
Telephone: (905) 468-4588 • Fax: (905) 468-2194 •
E-mail: uppercanadahotel@aol.com • Web site: www.uppercanadahotels.com •
Open year-round • Innkeepers: Howard Schweitzer and Maury Zeplowitz

LAKE HOUSE RESTAURANT AND LOUNGE

In the early 1800s, Abram Moyer, a Pennsylvania German and one of the first settlers in Vineland, built a sturdy home atop a knoll on the shores of Lake Ontario where it remains today, 150 years later, as a testament to his hard work, vision and stamina.

About twenty years ago it was converted into a restaurant and has since gone through several owners; however, few had taken advantage of its expansive view of the lake until the most recent owner, French-born Joseph Nahman. Nahman converted the small patio overlooking the lake into a larger deck as well as arranged the dining room to take the fullest advantage of the view.

It's still rustic, with exposed wood beamed ceilings and five fireplaces throughout. The acoustics are wonderful — you can actually hear yourself speak but not your neighbour's conversation. The cuisine, distinctly Mediterranean, is prepared by Chef Enzo Napoli, who makes incredibly light fresh pastas, thin crust pizzas, risottos and classic entrées of lamb, beef, chicken, veal and fish.

The progressive wine list is user-friendly (wines are grouped according to weight — light, medium, full), with representations from all the worlds major wine regions. In summer the patio overlooking the lake is a great spot to contemplate passing ships, watch the great hawks riding thermals or simply the enjoy pleasure of being in the presence of a great, great lake.

3106 North Service Road (QEW exit 55 or 57), Vineland, ON, L0R 2E0
Telephone: (905) 562-6777 • Fax: (905) 562-8287 •
E-mail: lakehouse@on.aibn.com • Open year-round • Lunch and dinner: daily
• Restaurateur: Joseph Nahman

LANGDON HALL

Langdon Hall was built in 1898 by Eugene Langdon Wilks, the great grandson of American financier John Jacob Astor. This impressive American Federal Revival house is located near Cambridge and situated among 200 acres of gardens and woodlands. Langdon Hall now consists of forty elegant guest rooms and thirteen suites, each with its own charm. Amenities include walking trails, lawn croquet, tennis courts, a swimming pool, sauna, whirlpool, exercise room and a full-service spa.

The dining room offers regional dishes and classical cuisine, served in an atmosphere of warmth and elegance overlooking the lily pond and gardens. The menu is rich in Langdon Hall's own products, such as honey, apples, vegetables and herbs, grown on the estate. Lunch and dinner are also available in the relaxed atmosphere of the lovely Wilks Bar, and in season on the terrace and patio.

R.R. 33, Cambridge, ON, N3H 4R8
Telephone: (519) 740-2100 or 1-800-268-1898 • Fax: (519) 740-8161 •
Open year-round • Innkeepers: Bill Bennett and Mary Beaton

THE LITTLE INN OF BAYFIELD

The Little Inn of Bayfield has been receiving guests with a warm, friendly welcome since the 1830s when it first opened its doors as a coach stop. Located in the picturesque heritage village of Bayfield, it's the perfect place to visit at any time of year. The Little Inn combines the charms of yesterday with the amenities of today. There are now twenty-nine rooms available at the Inn and no two are exactly alike. Many rooms have ensuite whirlpools and fireplaces.

From the lakes, streams, farms and fields of Huron County, and under the creativity of Chef Jean Jacques Chappuis, their imaginative menus are constantly changing.

Features include fresh, country-grown regional produce. Summer selections might include cold smoked Huron boar, oven-roasted Lake Huron whitefish, or a fresh ginger cream caramel. The wine list has received Awards of Excellence for its enormous selection for seven consecutive years from the *Wine Spectator*. Off-site guests are welcome for lunch and dinner.

Main Street, Bayfield, ON, N0M 1G0
Telephone: (519) 565-2611 or 1-800-565-1832 • Fax: (519) 565-5474 •
E-mail: innkeeper@littleinn.com • Web site: www.littleinn.com •
Open year-round • Innkeepers: Patrick and Gayle Waters

MARK PICONE AT VINELAND ESTATES WINERY RESTAURANT

In the heart of wine country, experience one of Niagara's premiere wine and culinary destinations. *Gourmet Magazine*, *Zagat Review* and *Toronto Life* have all recognized the restaurant as the quintessential wine country dining experience with an ambiance second to none.

Under the direction of Executive Chef Mark Picone, a talented team creates authentic Niagara cuisine with fresh seasonal ingredients. With fine dining inside or on the deck, guests can survey the breathtaking view overlooking the vineyards and Lake Ontario while enjoying the tantalizing creations of Chef Picone. The wine list features the award-winning wines of Vineland Estates. The menu changes seasonally.

3620 Moyer Road, Vineland, ON, L0R 2C0
Telephone: (905) 562-7088 or 1-888-846-3526 ext. 25 • Open year-round for lunch and dinner • Executive Chef: Mark Picone •
Winemaker: Brian Schmidt

THE OBAN INN

The Oban Inn has been a Niagara-on-the-Lake landmark for 170 years. It's beautifully situated where the waters of the Niagara River rush to join those of Lake Ontario and is surrounded by gorgeous English style gardens. The original inn was the home of Duncan Milloy from Oban, Scotland.

In 1992 a fire destroyed the building but within a year it was restored to its original splendor, with twenty-two rooms and all the amenities of an old English resort. The restaurant is open to the public for breakfast, lunch and dinner. Dinner in the dining room is a gracious white-linen affair. For lunch or after-theatre, regulars vie for space on the garden patio or at the bar.

In keeping with its British heritage, the menu features classic dishes such as slow-roasted prime rib and Yorkshire pudding or pan-seared Arctic char with rapini and kippered leek and potato fumet. The lounge serves great pub food such as bangers and mash, steak and ale pie, lamb shank and mashed potatoes or battered cod and fries.

160 Front Street, Niagara-on-the-Lake, ON, L0S 1J0
Telephone: (905) 468-2165 • Fax: (905) 468-4155 •
Open year-round • Lunch and dinner daily • Web site: www.vintageinns.com •
Restaurateur: Si Wai Lai

THE OLD PRUNE RESTAURANT

The Old Prune is set in a quiet Edwardian house, with tables clustered in three cozy rooms complemented by original art and large windows. A patio overlooks a secluded garden where one can take in the aromas of bread baking in the ovens and salmon smoking in the hothouse.

Using the finest and freshest ingredients raised by a dedicated community of organic farmers in the region, Chef Bryan Steele creates a cuisine of natural simplicity and abundant flavour. The service is professional. The wine list carries carefully selected vintages from right across the map and price range. Canadian wines are marketed with as much confidence as any others.

151 Albert Street, Stratford, ON, N5A 3K5
Telephone: (519) 271-5052 • Fax: (519) 271-4157 • E-mail: oldprune@cyg.net • Web site: www.oldprune.on.ca • Open May to October • Closed Monday • Dinner: Tuesday through Sunday • Lunch: Wednesday through Sunday • Restaurateurs: Marion Isherwood and Eleanor Kane

THE OTHER BROTHER'S RESTAURANT

The old Raymond's Sewing Machine Factory has been home to The Other Brother's Restaurant since October 1995. The restaurant has received many great reviews and accolades since it opened, particularly the Guelph Quality Award for service for four consecutive years.

The Other Brother's has a relaxed atmosphere with its glowing winter fireplace and beautiful summer patio. The kitchen team, Chef Mathew Brook and Sous Chef Kelly Pascoe, deliver food of the highest calibre from steaks and fresh lobster to confit of duck and a unique three-course fondue dinner.

The menu focuses on classically prepared dishes with some international flavours, and the decadent desserts all made in-house. The menu features such specialties as sesame smoked fillet of salmon, twice-cooked crispy skinned duck and cumin-crusted tuna. A three-course fondue dinner is served by reservation only.

The Other Brother's was honoured in 1997 as the "Best Fine Food Restaurant in North America" by Elan International Brands and was rated with two out of three stars — among the top sixty restaurants in the country — in Anne Hardy's *Where to Eat in Canada*.

37 Yarmouth Street, Guelph, ON, N1H 4G2
Telephone/fax: (519) 822-4465 • E-mail: info@otherbrothers.ca • Web site: www.otherbrothers.ca • Open year-round • Lunch: Tuesday through Friday • Dinner: Monday through Saturday • Restaurateurs: Sara Watson and Karim Ladhani

PELLER ESTATES WINERY RESTAURANT

Peller Estates Winery Restaurant, located on the outskirts of the village of Niagara-on-the-Lake, is simply gorgeous. Opened alongside the winery in 2001, it has offered outstanding dining from the very beginning, thanks to the inventive creations of Chef Jason Rosso. The setting is picturesque with vineyards surrounding the winery's periphery and the Niagara Escarpment in the distance. The splendid French-country inspired architecture is tastefully elegant in its simplicity and old-country charm.

Peller Estates wines, which are some of the finest in Ontario, comprise the wine list. Many of the selections are only available at the winery. Peller Estates was named after Andrew Peller, the founder of Andres Wines, who, only

forty years ago, came to Canada as a fifty-eight-year old Hungarian immigrant and opened a modest winery in British Columbia's Okanagan Valley. His entrepreneurial spirit built a successful business, which now includes Andres Wines, Hillebrand Estates and Peller Estates. It is the second largest wine company in Canada.

Peller Estates Winery Restaurant offers regional wine country cuisine that is highlighted by the abundance of fresh produce and products from the Niagara region. It's an experience you won't forget.

290 John Street East, Niagara-on-the-Lake, ON, L0S 1J0
Telephone: (905) 468-4678 or 1-888-673-5537 • Fax: (905) 468-1920 •
E-mail: info@peller.com • Web site: www.peller.com • Open year-round •
Lunch and dinner: daily • General Manager: Mark Torrence

THE PILLAR AND POST INN, SPA AND CONFERENCE CENTRE

The Pillar and Post Inn, Spa and Conference Centre is located in a quiet residential area, surrounded by gardens and only a five-minute walk from Niagara-on-the-Lake's main street. The Inn has been awarded the CAA/AAA Four Diamond Award for both accommodation and dining and is designated a Five Star Resort by Canada Select. Originally built in the late 1800s as a canning factory, since 1966 it has been gradually transformed into a luxurious county inn with 123 individually decorated cozy guest-rooms with fireplaces, four poster king-size beds and whirlpool tubs. The on-site European Spa and Health Club features thirteen massage, aesthetic and personal wellness services, indoor and outdoor swimming pools, an indoor hot tub and an outdoor hot spring.

Cozy fireside dining is set in the casually elegant Carriages and Cannery dining rooms where fresh produce from the Niagara region is offered. An extensive local and

imported wine selection is also available. Full country breakfasts and buffets are featured in both dining rooms.

King Street at John Street, P.O. Box 1011, Niagara-on-the-Lake, ON, L0S 1J0
Telephone: (905) 468-2123 • Fax: (905) 468-3551 •
Web site: www.vintageinns.com • Open year-round • Restaurateur: Si Wai Lai

PORT MANSION THEATRE RESTAURANT

This century-old property was once the focal point for sailors whose ships stopped for supplies along the old Welland Canal as they made their voyage from Lake Ontario to Lake Erie. It's a lavish old structure overlooking a marina where visible reminders of the three canals overlap in the Port Dalhousie harbour.

From the dining room terrace you can see old locks and the Custom's House. The Port Mansion is now a favourite summer spot for beach-goers, sailors, food lovers and theatre-goers. Besides being known for their seafood and their slow-roasted prime rib, an added bonus is a professional theatre, with no seat more than fifteen feet from the stage. Depending on their timing, diners can come for dinner and theatre or simply dinner, or simply theatre. There is a full season of scheduled productions.

The same group of owners also has a new cruise boat, *The Dalhousie Princess*, which is available for dinner cruises and parties.

12 Lakeport Road, Port Dalhousie, ON, L2N 4P5
Telephone: (905) 934-0575 • E-mail: dining@portmansion.com •
Web site: www.portmansion.com • Open daily

POW WOW

Pow Wow is aptly named — it has come to be known as a gathering place where friends meet and "where everybody knows your name." It was opened seven years ago by partners Greg Pearson and Richard Hall, who single-handedly transformed a venerated china shop, the old *Levitt's,* into an up-scale yet casual and friendly dinning establishment.

Chef Brian Corbierre soon joined as a partner, winning the hearts of diners with his global fusion cooking — using Asian, eastern Mediterranean and Italian influences to create such dishes as the Meze platter appetizer with roast garlic, pita triangles, humus and roasted red pepper puree, Komodo Dragon pasta and a piquant chicken dish he calls Angry Chicken. The lunch crowd also enjoys great sandwiches and salads. Dinner specials are offered daily but you can always find the chef's special beef tenderloin or a fresh fish dish on the menu.

Their wine list has a Niagara focus supplemented by New World classics with a reserve wine list available on request. Pow Wow's is 100% smoke free. It is also home to an art exhibition that changes monthly and features works from local artists through the Niagara Artists Centre.

Pow Wow also holds winemakers' dinners, monthly cooking classes and a wine club.

165 St. Paul Street, St. Catharines, ON, L2R 3M5
Telephone/Fax: (905) 688-3106 • E-mail: powwow12@cogeco.ca •
Open year-round • Lunch & dinner daily • Closed Sunday & holiday Mondays •
Restaurateurs: Richard Hall, Greg Pearson, Brian Corbierre

THE PRINCE OF WALES HOTEL

First established in 1864, the Prince of Wales Hotel is one of Niagara-on-the-Lake's most historic landmarks. Situated on the town's main street and awarded the CAA/AAA Four Diamond Award for both accommodation and dining, the Prince of Wales offers 112 elegant rooms, all retaining the charm of their Victorian origins. A "Secret Garden Spa" offers a full range of aesthetic and massage treatments and personal wellness care in charming treatment rooms.

The hotel's Escabeche restaurant is comfortable and gracious. The Prince's recipes are created with Niagara wines and daily-picked local farm ingredients. Menu items include a selection of regional and multi-continental cuisines including influences from Italy, California, the Mediterranean and France. Great fun is the Churchill Lounge, a traditional mahogany paneled library, which offers a versatile menu for those who wish to have a light meal.

A new addition to the hotel is the Taste of Niagara — Tapas Wine Bar, which introduces visitors to the Niagara wine experience through twelve appetizing tapas finger foods.

6 Picton Street, P.O. Box 1011, Niagara-on-the-Lake, ON, L0S 1J0
Telephone: (905) 468-3246 • Fax: (905) 468-5521 •
Web site: www.vintageinns.com • Open year-round • Restaurateur: Si Wai Lai

QUEEN'S LANDING INN & CONFERENCE RESORT

This stately Georgian-style mansion overlooking the scenic Niagara River is only minutes from the town's main street and the Shaw Festival Theatre. The 145 elegant guest rooms are individually decorated and feature cozy fireplaces and whirlpool baths.

The inn's Tiara restaurant is a dual-level circular room overlooking the beautiful Niagara River and the Niagara-

the restaurant are their traditional afternoon tea and delightful Sunday brunch.

14184 Niagara Parkway, P.O. Box 150, Niagara Falls, ON, L2E 6T2
Telephone: (905) 262-4274 • Fax: (905) 262-5557 •
E-mail: qhrest@niagaraparks.com • Web site: www.niagaraparks.com/
dining/queenstonres.php • Open: April through January for lunch and dinner daily and January through March for Sunday brunch • Manager: Lai Wah Chu

on-the-Lake Yacht Club. Elegant Georgian pillars support a magnificent stained glass ceiling. Exquisite fresh flowers abound. Executive Chef Stephen Treadwell creates a fusion of contemporary French cuisine with the bounty of fresh produce that only Niagara can offer. Chef Treadwell partners with local grower David Perkins from Wyndym Farm and incorporates the farm's heirloom and international vegetable varieties into his "New Niagara Cuisine" with such specialties as foi gras terrine with Concord grape jus, truffle dusted Provimi sweetbreads with Niagara pancetta with preserved quince in cardamom froth and Niagara peach preserves with vanilla bean and lime butter. Chef Treadwell is, indeed, one of the finest in Canada today.

155 Byron Street, P.O. Box 1180, Niagara-on-the-Lake, ON, L0S 1J0
Telephone: (905) 468-2195 • Fax: (905) 468-222 •
Web site: www.vintageinns.com • Open year-round • Restaurateur: Si Wai Lai

QUEENSTON HEIGHTS RESTAURANT

Queenston Heights Restaurant is located on the edge of the Niagara Escarpment 11 km north of the Falls in one of the most beautiful parks in Canada — Queenston Heights. Because of its high point along the Niagara River and above the hamlet of Queenston, it was a strategic area during the War of 1812. Many battles were fought on its grounds and are marked throughout the park, including the battle in which General Brock lost his life. To honour his valour the Brock Monument was erected and can be seen for miles and miles on both sides of the border!

The restaurant is located beside the Brock monument where the energetic can climb to the top for a breathtaking view of the countryside. Perhaps even better, however, is the magnificent view from the restaurant's dining room window of the Niagara River below as it meanders past rolling vineyards on its way to the mouth of Lake Ontario.

The food is also quite wonderful — highlighted by products that are grown in Niagara and complemented by an all-Niagara wine list, one of the most extensive in Ontario. In addition to lovely dining, two popular treats at

THE RESTAURANT AT PENINSULA RIDGE

Peninsula Ridge Estates Winery is one of Ontario's premium wine producers, noted for their Chardonnay and Sauvignon Blanc, plus one of Canada's very first Syrahs. Equally outstanding is their on-site restaurant located in the 1885 grand Victorian home of William D. Kitchen, the grandson of one of the area's early settlers. What is also significant about the site is its location just below the Niagara Escarpment, which serves as a romantic backdrop to the winery.

The restaurant has become known for its inventive presentations, the extraordinary depth of flavours achieved by Chef Ray Poitras through long reductions, the very freshest herbs and premium cuts of meat and poultry.

Particularly intriguing is their tasting menu, which consists of a series of five to six courses paired with Peninsula Ridge wines. They also host events such as winemakers' dinners plus a popular summer black tie "jazz on the ridge" fundraiser for a local hospital. It's a great place to learn more about wine, taste samples in the winery, then walk across to the restaurant for a lovely meal inside, or on the patio. Private parties can enjoy the Coach House beside the restaurant which is designed for large groups.

5600 King Street West, P.O. Box 550, Beamsville, ON, L0R 1B0
Telephone: (905) 563-0900 • Fax: (905) 563-0995 •
E-mail: info@peninsularidge.com • Web site: www.peninsularidge.com •
Open year-round Wednesday through Sunday • Restaurateur: Norman Beal

RISTORANTE GIARDINO

Situated on the main street in the historic village of Niagara-on-the-Lake, this heritage property housed the first Law Society of Upper Canada in 1797. The village, then called Newark, was the capital of a fledging nation. When the Law Society moved its headquarters, the building remained as a hotel and restaurant for many years. In 1989 the Dallavalle family from Modena, Italy, opened it as a venue for fine Italian food.

Today, Chefs Tullio Calvello and David Little make delicious fresh pastas, traditional risottos, tender Osso Bucco and Liver ala Veneziana, plus steak, pork and lamb dishes. They are also known for their marinated salmon and cheese soufflés, plus classical desserts such as Tiramisu and Pana Cotta.

The wine list is one of the most extensive in Niagara, with the majority of selections coming from Niagara or northern Italy.

142 Queen Street, Niagara-on-the-Lake, ON, L0S 1J0
Tel: (905) 468-3263 • Fax: (905) 468-7400 •
E-mail: giardino@niagara.com • Web site: www.gatehouse-niagara.com •
Open year-round • Lunch and dinner: daily • Restaurateurs: The Dallavalle Family

THE ROSELAWN DINING ROOM

The Roselawn Dining Room is an integral part of Port Colborne's arts and cultural scene. Located in a landmark Victorian mansion, Roselawn is dedicated to offering a wide range of events, concerts and theatre productions.

The menu is a la carte and provides a wide range of choices and specials, plus an all-Ontario wine list. There is live music on Friday and Saturday nights throughout the summer, plus a jazz series, readings with Canada's most well known authors, art exhibitions and a Victorian garden. Live professional theatre during the summer months rounds out a special visit to Roselawn.

P.O. Box 519, 296 Fielden Avenue, Port Colborne, ON, L3K 5X7
Telephone: (905) 834-7572 • Fax: (905) 834-4225 •
E-mail: info@niagara.com • Web site: www.roselawn.ca • Open year-round •
Dinner: Wednesday through Saturday • Lunch: Thursday and Friday, January through April, and Tuesday through Friday, May through December. Special bookings also available. • Executive Director: Fred Davies

RUNDLES

Rundles reflects the genuine passion for food and the arts of its soft-spoken owner, James Morris. It is located in a superbly decorated, summer-cool house, set by Stratford's pretty Avon River adrift with swans. The dining room is full of comforts with soft white cushions and numerous bouquets of beautiful flowers.

Rundles chef, Neil Baxter, has earned the attention of *Gourmet* and other important culinary magazines, with special tributes paid to his grilled vegetable terrine, crispy-skin *confit* of duck, beautiful grilled and cold-poached salmon, and seared shellfish coins. An international selection of carefully chosen wines complement the fine lunch and dinner menus.

9 Cobourg Street, Stratford, ON, N5A 3E4
Telephone: (519) 271-6442 • Fax: (519) 271-3279 • Open: May 24 to end of October • Closed Monday • Lunch: Wednesday, Saturday and Sunday • Dinner: Tuesday through Sunday • Restaurateur: James Morris

STONE MAIDEN INN

The Stone Maiden Inn, built in 1872, is named for the carved stone figureheads which adorn the front hallway. This special bed-and-breakfast, located two blocks from downtown Stratford, has a fresh country atmosphere yet preserves its early Victorian elegance. Its fourteen comfortable guest rooms are decorated in soft colours with cozy quilts, pillows and antiques. Fireplaces, whirlpool baths, and refrigerators are found in some rooms.

In the morning, guests can enjoy early coffee or tea in their rooms, followed by a bountiful breakfast in the dining room. In the afternoon, they can relax in the comfortable parlour or outside on the sun porch where complimentary beverages and other treats are offered.

123 Church Street, Stratford, ON, N5A 2R3
Telephone: (519) 271-7129 • Fax: (519) 271-4615 •
E-mail: smaiden@execulink.com • Web site: www.stonemaideninn.com •
Open: April through December • Innkeepers: Elaine and Jim Spencer

TERROIR LA CACHETTE RESTAURANT AND WINE BAR AT STREWN WINERY

This is the Niagara incarnation of the original La Cachette in Elora, Ontario. There it was recognized in *Where To Eat in Canada* and *Toronto Life Restaurant Guide* as one of the best.

When Chef Alain Levesque and his wife Patricia Keys re-located in Niagara in August 2000 into the same complex as Strewn Winery, they acknowledged their winery affiliation by adding the term "Terroir," which implies the entire environment in which the grapes on the vine are transformed into wine, to their name.

The base of their cuisine is still Provençal with vegetarian, seafood, chicken, pork and beef dishes. The dining room overlooks Four Mile Creek and the surrounding countryside. The building was originally one of Niagara's largest fruit canning operations and a focal point of community life.

In a short time they have established their restaurant as one of Niagara's real dining treasures. They also host winemakers' dinners, plus innovative events throughout the year.

1339 Lakeshore Road, Niagara-on-the-Lake, ON, L0S 1J0
Telephone: (905) 468-1222 • E-mail: tricia@lacachette.com •
Web site: www.lacachette.com • Open for lunch and dinner daily •
Closed: Monday and Tuesdays from November to the end of May •
Restauranteurs: Patricia Keys and Alain Levesque

WELLINGTON COURT RESTAURANT

Located in the heart of Niagara's wine region, Wellington Court is Edwardian in style on the outside. Inside, the intimate jazz-filled dining room offers a quaint setting in which to enjoy the superb creations of one of Niagara's premier chefs, Eric Peacock. Eric uses only the freshest local ingredients to present a meal as pleasing to the eye as it is to the palate.

Established in 1985 by Claudia Peacock, Wellington Court maintains a strong reputation for excellent fine dining and service in a relaxed atmosphere. It has enjoyed thirteen years of recognition in Anne Hardy's *Where to Eat in Canada*.

11 Wellington Street, St. Catharines, ON, L2R 5P5
Telephone: (905) 682-5518 • Fax: (905) 684-6350 •
E-mail: epeacock@vaxxine.com • Web site: www.wellington-court.com •
Open year-round • Lunch and Dinner: Tuesday through Saturday •
Restaurateur: Claudia Peacock

of exquisitely presented dishes, including fresh seafood, lamb, beef, and vegetarian dishes. All sauces, dressings and desserts are homemade. Niagara regional wines (VQA) are offered to complement the Wildflower's menu.

219 Highway 20 East, Fonthill, ON, L0S 1E6
Telephone: (905) 892-6167 • Fax: (905) 892-4650 • Open year-round • Lunch and dinner: Tuesday to Saturday • Sunday, bunch only • Seasonal: April to October, Sunday dinner • Reservations recommended • Restaurateurs: Wolfgang Sterr and Emily Schild

WOOLFYS AT WILDWOOD RESTAURANT

Woolfys at Wildwood Restaurant is situated on the outskirts of the town of St. Marys, in the heart of the Perth County countryside. It is close to the Stratford Festival theatres and therefore hosts an international clientele.

The menu offers modern and traditional dishes, changing daily and featuring local organic produce. The dining room has a warm, casual ambiance, and the service is attentive and professional, hosted by Mary Woolf, the wife of chef Chris Woolf. The wine list is chosen from regular tastings and features Canadian and international wines and beers.

R.R. # 2, St. Marys, ON, N4X 1C5
Telephone: (519) 349-2467 • E-mail: woolfy@woolfys.com • Open: February 14 through December 31 • February 14 through May 31 • Dinner: Friday and Saturday • June 1 through September 30 • Breakfast, Lunch and Dinner: Tuesday through Saturday • October 1 through December 31 • Dinner: Friday and Saturday • Restaurateurs: Chris and Mary Woolf

THE WESTOVER INN

The Westover Inn began as a limestone Victorian mansion, built in 1867 by William and Joseph Hutton as their family home. One hundred and thirty-six years later, the inn offers twenty-two charming guest rooms set on nineteen acres of landscaped grounds. It is located just twelve miles from Stratford, in the town of St. Marys. Over the last sixteen years, The Westover Inn has evolved into a destination for Stratford Festival actors, such as Christopher Plummer.

The Westover features two unique dining rooms and an outdoor patio serving award-winning cuisine. The Westover's three executive chefs have shaped the inn's superb menu around locally grown ingredients.

300 Thomas Street, St. Marys, ON, N4X 1B1
Telephone: (519) 284-2977 or 1-800-268-8243 • Fax: (519)284-4043 • Web site: www.westoverinn.com • Open year-round • Innkeepers: Julie Docker-Johnson and Stephen McCotter

THE WILDFLOWER RESTAURANT

The Wildflower is an intimate small restaurant located just outside of Fonthill at the corner of Rice Road and Highway 20. The cozy forty-eight-seat dining room is surrounded by large bay windows filled with plants, homegrown herbs and greenery. Dried wildflowers hang from the wooden rafters creating a warm and inviting atmosphere.

Because the Wildflower is located in the heart of the Niagara region, Chef Wolfgang Sterr uses locally sourced products wherever possible. The menu consists of a variety

Angels Gate Winery
Rosé, 2002, 56
Appetizers, 9-29
Artichoke Strudel, 25
Blackshop Marinated Salmon, 14
Cha Gio, 15
Clover Honey Roasted Quail with
Peach Gravy on Ruby Chard, 20
Cucumber Goat Cheese Torte, 29
Duck Crêpes, 19
Goat Cheese Soufflé with Lettuces
and Marinated Vegetables, 26-27
Joe Speck Farms Quail Mousseline
with Balsamic Caramelized
Onions and Cheese Crisps, 6-17
Mini Pancakes (Poffertjes) with
Lamb Croquettes and Blueberry
Chutney, 22-23
Mussels Steamed in Thai Citrus
and Coconut Broth, 10
Smoked Chicken Spring Rolls, 18
Smoked Trout Rillette, 12
Stuffed Portobello Mushrooms on
Mixed Greens, 28
Thai Shrimp, 13
Tomato Basil Tart, 24
Artichokes,
Artichoke Strudel, 25
Crab Salad with Artichokes, 44-45

Bailey's Restaurant, 4, 13, 77, 108
Beef,
Steak au Poivre, 77
Bench Bistro at EastDell Estates
Winery, The, 4, 108
Benmiller Inn & Spa, 4, 56, 68, 109
Bhima's Warung International, 4, 15,
70, 109
Birchwood Estate Wines,
Gewürztraminer Riesling, 2000,
76
Cabernet Franc Icewine, 2000, 95
Blackshop Restaurant & Lounge, 4,
14, 64, 110
Breads & Breakfast Foods, 99-107
Adelaide's Nova Scotia Brown
Bread, 106
Country Apple and Apricot
Muffins, 104
Decadent French Toast, 100
Muesli Bread, 107

Scones with Niagara-on-the-Lake
Clotted Cream, 101
Scrumptious Egg Casserole, 102
Smoked Bacon Corn Bread with
Root Cellar Vegetable Slather,
105
Sunrise Casserole, 102

Casa Mia Ristorante & Bar, 4, 110
Cave Spring Cellars,
Chardonnay Reserve, 2000, 80
Chardonnay, 2002, 19
Dry Riesling, 2002, 36, 44
Gamay Noir Reserve, 2002, 24
Off Dry Riesling, 2002, 29
Reserve Chardonnay, 1999, 62
Riesling Indian Summer Select
Late Harvest, 2000, 70
Riesling Reserve, 2002, 12
Château des Charmes,
Aligoté, 2000, 40
Late Harvest Riesling, 2000, 84
St. David's Bench Chardonnay,
2000, 54
Chicken,
Bakers' Chicken Vermicelli, 64
Breast of Chicken with Goat
Cheese and Sun-Dried Tomato
Jus, 67
Grain-Fed Chicken with Herbed
Cream Cheese and Fresh Tomato
Sauce, 66
Pan-Seared Breast of Chicken
with Braised Ruby Chard and
Rhubarb Wine, 65
Smoked Chicken Spring Rolls, 18
Church Restaurant, The, 4, 26, 60,
90, 110-11
Cilento Wines,
Sauvignon Blanc Reserve, 2001,
41
Colio Estate Winery,
Late Harvest Vidal, 2000, 45
Crab,
Cha Gio, 15
Crab Salad with Artichokes, 44-45
Creekside Estate Winery,
Sauvignon Blanc, 2002, 27

Da Caruso Ristorante, 63
Daniel Lenko Estate Winery, 10

Gewürztraminer, 2002, 10
Desserts, 83-97
Apple Raisin Cake with
Homemade Maple Walnut Ice
Cream, 89
Brandy and Vanilla Custard on
Three-Berry Compote, 92-93
Clafoutis, 86
Creamy Lemon Delight with
Cointreau-Marinated
Strawberries, 88
Crème Brûlée with Toffeed
Strawberries, 90-91
Hazelnut Cappucino Torte, 87
Hillebrand Estate's Trius Icewine
Truffles, 94
Lemon and Mascapone Mousse in
Phyllo, 84
Maple Walnut Ice Cream, 89
Raspberries with Mango Sorbet,
96
Riesling-Marinated Berries with
Bread and Butter Pudding, 95
Thyme Ice Cream, 97
Toffeed Strawberries, 91
Devlin's Country Bistro & Catering,
4, 25, 111
Duck,
Barbecued Breast of Duck
Accented with Coconut &
Accompanied with Grilled
Vegetables, 68-69
Bebek Betutu (Roast Duck), 70
Duck Crêpes, 19

EastDell Estates,
Vidal Icewine, 1999, 89
Edgewater Manor Restaurant, 4, 111
Eggs,
Scrumptious Egg Casserole, 102
Sunrise Casserole, 102
Elm Hurst Inn, 4, 62, 71, 112
Elora Mill Inn, 4, 19, 112
Entrées, 51-81
Baked Atlantic Salmon with
Lemon Cream Sauce and
Creamy Risotto, 58-59
Bakers' Chicken Vermicelli, 64
Barbecued Breast of Duck
Accented with Coconut &
Accompanied with Grilled

Vegetables, 68-69
Bebek Betutu (Roast Duck), 70
Breast of Chicken with Goat
  Cheese and Sun-Dried Tomato
  Jus, 67
Cheese Soufflé, 80
Fillet of Lake Trout with Morels and
  Fiddleheads on Linguine, 53-54
Grain-Fed Chicken with Herbed
  Cream Cheese and Fresh Tomato
  Sauce, 66
Grilled Pork Tenderloin with
  Riesling Cream Corn and
  Asparagus Crispin Apple Fritters,
  74-75
Grilled Provimi Veal Chop with a
  Farce of Various Mushrooms,
  Spinach and Asiago Cheese, 72
Grilled Tuna with Chilled Olive
  Salad, 56
Grilled Vegetable and Tofu Tortes,
  81
Grilled Venison Chop with Wilted
  Arugula, Radiccio, Endive and
  Walnut Bread, 79
Linguine Mare, 63
Linguine with Shrimps and
  Scallops, 62
Medallions of Lamb with Apricots
  and Peppercorn Honey Glaze, 76
Pan-Seared Breast of Chicken
  with Braised Ruby Chard and
  Rhubarb Wine, 65
Pork Tenderloin with Four
  Peppercorn Crust and Apple
  Calvados Jus, 71
Salmon Monette, 60-61
Steak au Poivre, 77
Striped Sea Bass with Lemon
  Pepper Butter Sauce and Corn
  and Potato Risotto, 52-53
Trout Baked in Apple Cider, 57
Enver's Restaurant, 4, 80,112
Epicurean, The, 4, 47, 112-13

Featherstone Estate Winery,
  Gewürztraminer, 2002, 13

Glenerin Inn, The, 4, 36, 41, 76, 113
Goat Cheese,
  Cucumber Goat Cheese Torte, 29

Warm Goat Cheese Salad and
  Grilled Vegetables with Roasted
  Garlic Dressing, 46
Goat Cheese Soufflé with Lettuces
  and Marinated Vegetables, 26-27

Harbour Estates Winery,
  Riesling, 2000, 60
Harvest Estates Winery,
  Strawberry Rhubarb, 65
Henry of Pelham Family Estate
  Winery,
  Baco Noir Reserve, 2000, 79
  Rosé, 2002, 47
  Pinot Noir, 1998, 14
  Special Select Late Harvest Vidal,
  2000, 68
Hernder Estate Winery,
  Off-Dry Riesling, 2002, 15
Hillebrand Estates Winery,
  Lakeshore Chardonnay, 2000, 74
  Riesling Icewine, 1998, 97
  Trius Brut, 17
  Trius Icewine, 94
  Trius Red, 1998, 77
Hillebrand Estates Winery
  Restaurant, 4, 16, 74, 94, 113

Idlewyld Inn, 4, 106-07, 114
Inn on the Twenty, 4, 24, 29, 114
Inniskillin Wines,
  Auxerrois, 2002, 18, 42
  Cabernet Franc Reserve, 1999, 72
  Chardonnay, 2002, 28
  Pinot Noir Reserve, 2000, 64

Jackson-Triggs Niagara Estate
  Winery,
  Chardonnay, 2002, 34
Janet Lynn's Bistro, 4, 46, 114

Kettle Creek Inn, 4, 65, 87, 115
Keystone Alley Café, 4, 66, 89, 115
Kiely Inn and Tapestries Restaurant,
  The, 4, 32, 42, 52, 115
Konzelmann Estate Winery,
  Golden Vintage Vidal, 2001, 20
  Pinot Blanc, 2000, 52

Lailey Vineyard,
  Pinot Noir, 2002, 22

Lake House Restaurant and Lounge,
  4, 116
Lakeview Cellars,
  Dry Riesling, 2002, 35
Lakewinds, 101
Lamb,
  Medallions of Lamb with Apricots
  and Peppercorn Honey Glaze, 76
  Mini Pancakes (Poffertjes) with
  Lamb Croquettes and Blueberry
  Chutney, 22-23
Langdon Hall, 4, 57, 116
Little Inn of Bayfield, The, 4, 53, 88,
  116-17
Lobster,
  Lobster Cakes, 35

Malivoire Wine Company,
  Chardonnay, 2000, 67
Marc Picone at Vineland Estates
  Winery Restaurant, 4, 22, 35, 117
Marynissen Estates,
  Pinot Noir, Butler's Grant
  Vineyard, 2000, 81
Mushrooms,
  Stuffed Portobello Mushrooms on
  Mixed Greens, 28
  Warm Scallop and Portobello
  Salad, 40
Mussels,
  Mussel Chowder with Root
  Vegetables and Fresh Dill, 34
  Mussels Steamed in Thai Citrus
  and Coconut Broth, 10

Oban Inn, The, 4, 117
Old Prune Restaurant, The, 4, 12,
  86, 118
Other Brother's Restaurant, The, 4,
  97, 118

Pasta,
  Bakers' Chicken Vermicelli, 64
  Linguine Mare, 63
  Linguine with Shrimps and
  Scallops, 62
Pelee Island Winery,
  Riesling Icewine, 2000, 86
Peller Estates Winery Restaurant, 4,
  118-19
Pillar and Post Inn, Spa and

Conference Centre, The, 4, 20, 105, 119
Pillitteri Estates Winery, Pinot Grigio, 2000, 32
Pork,
    Cha Gio, 15
    Grilled Pork Tenderloin with Riesling Cream Corn and Asparagus Crispin Apple Fritters, 74-75
    Pork Tenderloin with Four Peppercorn Crust and Apple Calvados Jus, 71
Port Mansion Theatre Restaurant, 4, 119
Pow Wow, 4, 120
Prince of Wales Hotel, The, 4, 28, 48, 79, 120

Quail,
    Clover Honey Roasted Quail with Peach Gravy on Ruby Chard, 20
    Joe Speck Farms Quail Mousseline with Balsamic Caramelized Onions and Cheese Crisps, 16-17
Queen's Landing Inn & Conference Resort, 4, 95, 104, 120-21
Queenston Heights Restaurant, 4, 121

Reif Estate,
    Special Select Late Harvest Vidal, 2000, 90
Restaurant at Peninsula Ridge, The, 4, 121
Risotto,
    Creamy Risotto, 59
    Potato Risotto, 53
Ristorante Giardino, 4, 122
Roselawn Dining Room, The, 4, 122
Rundles, 4, 44, 96, 123

Salads, 39-48
    Candy Cane Beet and Feta Cheese Salad, 45
    Chilled Olive Salad, 56
    Crab Salad with Artichokes, 44-45
    Hearts of Romaine with Caramelized Onion Vinaigrette, 42
    Mixed Greens with Poppy Seed

Dressing, 47
    Salad Deanna, 41
    Vodka Caesar Salad, 48
    Warm Goat Cheese Salad and Grilled Vegetables with Roasted Garlic Dressing, 46
    Warm Scallop and Portobello Salad, 40
Salmon,
    Baked Atlantic Salmon with Lemon Cream Sauce and Creamy Risotto, 58-59
    Blackshop Marinated Salmon, 14
    Salmon Monette, 60-61
Sauces,
    Benmiller Inn's Barbecue Sauce, 69
    Blueberry Chutney, 22
    Fish Mayonnaise, 41
    Fresh Tomato Sauce, 66
    Green Peppercorn Butter, 77
    Lemon Cream Sauce, 58
    Nuoc Cham, 15
    Onion Vinaigrette, 42
    Peach Gravy, 21
    Roasted Garlic Dressing, 46
    Lemon Pepper Butter, 52
Scallops,
    Warm Scallop and Portobello Salad, 40
    Linguine with Shrimps and Scallops, 62
Schoolhouse Country Inn Restaurant, The, 18, 40
Sea Bass,
    Striped Sea Bass with Lemon Pepper Butter Sauce and Corn and Potato Risotto, 52-53
Shrimp,
    Thai Shrimp, 13
    Linguine with Shrimps and Scallops, 62
Soups, 31-37
    Cream of Spinach and Feta Soup, 36
    Mussel Chowder with Root Vegetables and Fresh Dill, 34
    Niagara Gazpacho, 37
    Oriental Bouillabaisse, 32
    Roasted Pear and Sweet Potato Bisque with Lobster Cakes, 35
Southbrook Winery,

Blush, 2000, 71
    Chardonnay Triomphe, 1999, 46
    Framboise D'Or, 92, 96
Stone Maiden Inn, 4, 100, 102, 123
Stoney Ridge Cellars,
    Riesling Reserve, 1999, 63
    Sauvignon Blanc, 2002, 37
Strewn Winery,
    Two Vines Riesling Gewürztraminer, 1999, 57

Terroir La Cachette Restaurant and Wine Bar at Strewn Winery, 4, 124
Thomas & Vaughan Vintners, Pinot Gris, 2001, 66
Tofu,
    Grilled Vegetable and Tofu Tortes, 81
Trout,
    Fillet of Lake Trout with Morels and Fiddleheads on Linguine, 53-54
    Smoked Trout Rillette, 12
    Trout Baked in Apple Cider, 57
Tuna,
    Grilled Tuna with Chilled Olive Salad, 56

Veal,
    Grilled Provimi Veal Chop with a Farce of Various Mushrooms, Spinach and Asiago Cheese, 72
Venison,
    Grilled Venison Chop with Wilted Arugula, Radiccio, Endive and Walnut Bread, 79
Vineland Estates Winery,
    Dry Riesling, 2002, 25
    Pinot Gris, 2000, 48

Wellington Court Restaurant, 4, 10, 37, 84, 124
Westover Inn, The, 4, 34, 72, 92, 125
Wildflower Restaurant, The, 4, 58, 81, 125
Willow Heights Estate Winery,
    Chardonnay Stefanik Vineyard Reserve, 1999, 58
Woolfys at Wildwood Restaurant, 4, 45, 67, 125